Wood in American Life, 1776-2076

Madison, Wisconsin

W. G. Youngquist and H. O. Fleischer

WOOD
in American Life

1776-2076

Forest Products Research Society

Title page: The majestic eagle, a symbol of freedom, courage, and pride, expresses the independence the colonist loved so dearly. The *Great Republic* figurehead (62" x 31") adorned the bow of the largest merchant vessel ever built in the United States and launched in 1853. The eagle was adopted as our national emblem in 1782, over 6 years after the Revolution. (Photo courtesy Mystic Seaport, Mystic, Conn.)

Opposite page: Pine tree shilling courtesy Bowers and Ruddy Galleries, Los Angeles, California.

End sheet photo by W. G. Youngquist

"What better thing than a tree to portray the wealth of our country." Joseph Jenks

ACKNOWLEDGMENTS

This account of wood use in America is based on such a wide variety of old and current source materials that meaningful acknowledgments are most difficult. Special thanks, however, are extended to Lawrence S. Klepp, a free lance writer from Madison, Wisconsin, for his patient and thorough historical research. Most of the early source material is from the library of the State Historical Society of Wisconsin, Madison, Wisconsin. A number of staff members of the U.S. Forest Products Laboratory in Madison, Wisconsin, also provided important source materials.

In addition to this wealth of information, the authors have drawn on their own experiences and knowledge obtained in life-long careers in forest products research. H. O. Fleischer served as director of the U.S Forest Products Laboratory until his retirement in July of 1975. W. G. Youngquist served as assistant to the director until his retirement in December of 1974. The authors are solely responsible for opinions expressed and for the predictions of the role of wood in America's future.

In 1976 the U.S. Forest Products Laboratory published, under the same authorship, a limited number of copies of an earlier version of this story as part of the bicentennial celebration of the United States of America.

FOREWORD

"What better thing than a tree to portray the wealth of our country!" remarked Joseph Jenks, designer of an early American coin, the pine tree shilling of Massachusetts. This book is dedicated to that theme. For then as now, and into the distant future, America depends on its forest resources far more than most realize. Today's generation of Americans, overwhelmed with fumes and asphalt, recognizes the uplifting effect on the human spirit of the primeval forest; and so it should. Early Americans understandably followed a practical philosophy which equated progress with the removal of the all-overshadowing forest, an obstacle to their plans. Yet the ingenious settlers found ways of using the forest and its products to support life, civilization, and progress. While many were penniless, they provided for their comforts and necessities in ways unknown to their European parents. As a result of their labors the forest yielded cabins and canoes, firewood and furniture, bowls and baskets, medicines and maple sugar, spruce beer and bridges, charcoal and carriages, barrels and bed frames, plow shares and ships, pipe organs and outhouses, cradles and coffins.

The forest means many things to many people. Yet this book examines only one material product of the forest—wood. Because of its versatility, and because it is America's most important renewable material resource, wood will continue to play an important role in American life long after other resources have been exhausted.

Changes and developments in wood usage make up a little-known but important part of U. S. history. This part of that continuing legacy deals with wood use in America during four periods: the founding in 1776, the centennial in 1876, the bicentennial in 1976, and projected to the year 2076. The story of wood that emerges from colonial times to the present is many faceted—from wanton waste to wise use. Each use of wood must be evaluated for wisdom on the basis of the social, political, and economic conditions existing at that particular time. Readily apparent, however, is the fact that the practices of the past and the present will not meet the requirements of the future. To ensure the United States an adequate supply of wood for future needs, including those of recreation and pleasure, will require both planning and foresight.

W. G. Youngquist
H. O. Fleischer

CONTENTS

PART 1

WOOD IN THE NEW NATION

The white clapboard St. John's Church in Richmond, Virginia, where Patrick Henry gave his famous address to the Second Virginia Convention in March of 1775. Significantly, Henry also said, "We are not weak if we make proper use of those means which the God of nature hath placed in our power." (Courtesy Valentine Museum, Richmond, Va., ca. 1920)

1776

Americans today find it difficult to visualize the United States as it existed in colonial times. Vast tracts of uninhabited forest, an abundance of wild animals, and a multitude of natural resources covered the land. A visitor to the Thirteen Original States would have discovered a sparsely populated, mostly rural nation with the wilderness never far away.

In 1776 nine out of ten Americans lived in the country. The largest city, Philadelphia, had a population of only 34,000; New York, 22,000; and Boston, 15,000. About 2.5 million Americans were scattered along the eastern seaboard from Maine to the border of Florida. In the North most Americans lived on compact, almost self-sufficient farms or in small villages. In the South some lived on great plantations and produced tobacco and other staple crops; some lived on small farms.

The towns, in both North and South, prospered and, to a large extent, depended on the export and trade of agricultural commodities. The towns also served as centers for a variety of small industries and crafts. Maritime industries were concentrated in New England; glassware factories, rum distilleries, iron foundries, sawmills, and other industries could be found throughout the states.

The population of both town and country was increasing rapidly, because of the large families standard at that time—an average of about eight children—and because of the waves of

Family life from cooking to conversation centered around the hearth. Some early fireplaces were designed for logs 2 to 3 feet thick. (Courtesy Old Sturbridge Village, Sturbridge, Mass.)

immigration from the Old World. Probably two-thirds of Americans in 1776, excluding native Indians, were immigrants or the children of immigrants. Germans and Scotch-Irish settled in Pennsylvania; Dutch in New York; English, Irish, Swedes, Scots, Swiss, and French scattered throughout the country; and African blacks, brought by force as slaves, settled mostly in the South. All added ethnic differences to the geographical and religious differences that led the British government, among others, to assume that the states could not cooperate, let alone form a lasting union. Common opposition to the British and a growing sense of American identity did overcome differences between the states, but not without frequent difficulties.

In 1776 about a fourth of the population lived in the "back country" away from the older coastal settlements. The frontier society, a cradle of differences, was already contributing distinctive social customs, dress, speech, and political interests to American life. Settlers moved westward along the rivers, crossing the Appalachian Mountains into the Ohio Valley. Woods and prairies extending from the mountains west to the Mississippi were still mainly inhabited by Indian tribes and French fur trappers. Spain held the French-speaking town of New Orleans and the trans-Mississippi West. In the Southwest there was a long established Spanish-Indian culture, and Spanish religious orders were spreading missions along the California coast. On the Great Plains the Plains Indians enjoyed their Golden Age, using the descendants of Spanish horses to create a prosperous nomadic culture based on buffalo hunting.

Use and Abuse of Forests

The West in 1776 remained almost uninterrupted wilderness. Even in most of the 13 original states the dominant geographical feature was a dense wilderness of forest, not farmland. When the settlers arrived, the continuous eastern forest, extending from Maine to Florida and west to the Mississippi Valley, encompassed more than a million square miles. For the European colonists from lands with only a few scattered woods left, the dark and impenetrable forest that crowded the seashore and harbored Indians and wild animals must have been an implacable, haunting presence. But they quickly took a practical view. In 1630 the Reverend Frances Higginson wrote:

For Wood there is no better in the World . . . here being foure sorts of oke differeing in the leafe, timber, and colour, all excellent good. There is also good ash, elme, willow, birch, beech, saxafras, juniper, cipres, cedar, spruce, pine, firre, that will yeeld abundance of turpentine, pitch, tarre, masts, and other materials for building of ships and houses.[1]

From the time of the first settlers, trees had been cut for ships and houses, but there were more trees than could be used. For the colonists the forest, as much an obstacle as a resource, had to be cleared quickly for planting crops. Cutting trees was slow and laborious for large areas, and it was dangerous. Only expert felling avoided accidents. The settlers frequently adopted the Indian method of girdling trees, stripping a ring of bark from a tree. This killed the tree, literally "cut its throat!" Crops could be planted around the leafless trees; the timber would eventually rot and could be dragged away. In 1776 this practice was still common as testified by British officer Thomas Anbury. In his letters he describes vast fields full of great, dead trees, with large branches and whole trunks that continually fell to the ground with a horrible crash.[2]

A method of clearing still more wasteful and dangerous than girdling, also adopted from the Indians, was deliberate burning of forests. Farmers would burn the forest not only to clear land, but simply to get rid of insects and animals or to encourage the growth of grass. Hunters left their campfires burning against trees. Pioneers thought no more of burning a forest than of burning a weed patch. In 1762 a fire burned 50 miles from the White Mountains of New Hampshire to the Maine coast and consumed sawmills, farms, and cattle. Throughout the summer in the Virginia mountains there were numerous large fires mostly caused by teamsters who neglected to extinguish their campfires.

Americans today are so well versed in conservation and the aesthetic value of forests that it is difficult to realize the antagonism and fear with which most early Americans regarded the wilderness. Aside from being an obstacle to the farmer, the forest was associated with hostile Indians, dangerous animals, insects, and fevers. Except in parts of New England and in areas of Pennsylvania settled by Germans, a farmer often cut down every tree in sight of his cabin leaving not even one for shade or decoration.

The practical implications of the waste were impatiently brushed aside. When questions of conservation arose, people asserted that the vast American forests were inexhaustible. This myth of inexhaustibility of the forest proved itself to be almost inexhaustible. It is not surprising that the myth got started. Most colonists immigrated from the British Isles, where a few hundred acres of woods were a great forest; in America they found forests many times the size of England itself. These attitudes toward the forests prevailed for countless years. Yet in some localities shortages of wood started local conservation measures. A few perceptive people anticipated more serious shortages. Because it served as the primary fuel and the main raw material of 18th century America, wood was rapidly consumed even by the relatively small population.

In 1720 Daniel Neal in his *History of New England* estimated that 6 million (evidently lineal) feet of timber were cut each year in New England.[3] Later in the century, Benjamin Rush, in a letter to Thomas Jefferson, wrote that 6,000 maple trees were destroyed or used as firewood in clearing the average New York or Pennsylvania farm. Coal was not yet mined in large quantities in America, and the Revolutionary War cut off the small supply from England. So, the New England home needed from 20 to 60 cords of wood yearly for heat (one cord equals a stack of wood 4 ft. wide, 8 ft. long, and 4 ft. high). The citizens of Massachusetts, then, would have used more than 750,000 cords a year for firewood, mostly oak, ash, hickory, and hard maple. The Franklin stove had just been introduced into American homes. One of Benjamin Franklin's most valuable inventions, it heated a house much more efficiently than did the traditional large open fireplace; therefore, it consumed less wood.

In Rhode Island all trees suitable for firewood had been cut by 1738; then wood had to be brought by boat from Long Island and elsewhere. No longer were forests very close to any of the coastal cities to provide fuel, and the long transportation often drove the prices beyond what the poor could afford. In New York where more than 20,000 cords of wood were annually burned in fireplaces and stoves, a newspaper in 1761 called the situation alarming, and stated, "Wood grows scarcer and dearer every year, whilst the demand increases with the growth of the City."[4]

Boston obtained most of its firewood by boat from Penobscot,

Maine, but also depended on wood brought overland by cart or sled. In both Boston and New York firewood peddlers from the country often fleeced city dwellers, prompting passage of laws to regulate price and quality. In New York and Philadelphia as prices rose, charitable organizations distributed firewood to the poor. This could be called America's first fuel crisis.

Plenty of forests remained, of course, but were in increasingly remote areas not easily logged. By 1750 the forests in the major river valleys of the East had been exhausted. Because of poor transportation, forests away from rivers or in mountainous country remained inaccessible. Later, to be sure, these forests could be logged, so there was no impending danger of the absolute exhaustion of the eastern forest. However, for those who cared, the immediate situation held ominous aspects. In 1763 John Bartram, calling attention to the clearing of Pennsylvania lands "quite to the mountains" said, "What our people will do for fencing and firewood fifty years hence, I can't imagine."[5] By the end of the 18th century warnings multiplied. Fearing for the future of the American Navy, John Jay wrote to President Washington, "There is some reason to apprehend that masts and ship-timber will, as cultivation advances, become scarce, unless some measures be taken to prevent their waste, or provide for the preservation of a sufficient fund of both."[6]

In 1798 an article in the *Weekly Magazine* entitled "On the Importance of Preserving Our Forests" urged that setting fires be regulated by law, that forest preserves be established, and that forests with aesthetic as well as practical value be cared for along rights-of-way and in scenic areas. A German physician and forester, Johann David Schoepf, toured the country after the War of Independence and summarized the situation acutely:

> In America there is no sovereign right over forests and game, no forest service. Whoever holds new land . . . controls it as his exclusive possession . . . . It will not easily come about therefore that, as a strict statutory matter, farmers and landowners will be taught how to manage their forests so as to leave for their grandchildren a bit of wood over which to hang the teakettle. Experience and necessity must here take the place of magisterial provision.[7]

Experience and necessity, however, were slow in teaching

conservation to people living under the spell of a myth of forest inexhaustibility.

The first conservation law in America was passed by Plymouth Colony in 1626. To prevent inconveniences that might befall a plantation needing timber, the sale or transport of timber out of the colony was prohibited without the approval of the governor and council. In several colonies a series of laws followed, regulating cutting and distributing timber. William Penn, in founding Pennsylvania in 1681, stipulated that 1 acre of forest be left for every 5 acres cleared, and that special care to taken to preserve oak.

The British government tried to impose laws preserving large white pines for shipmasts, but these laws were widely resented and flagrantly violated. To prevent erosion Massachusetts tried to regulate cutting timber on beaches. Legislation regulating fires became common throughout the colonies. In 1772 New York enacted a minimum cutting diameter to insure reforestation. But the laws were difficult to enforce, especially in the back country where attitudes of carelessness and hostility toward the forest prevailed. Nevertheless, the laws reflect an early awareness of a need for a conservation policy, an awareness that finally developed into the conservation movement and the improvements in forest management of the 19th and 20th centuries.

Lumbering in 1776

The prominence of the forest in early American life encouraged development of the lumber industry. Appropriately, the word "lumber" received its present meaning from the colonists. In all new settlements lumbering was on a small scale using primitive methods. Because of transportation problems, early lumbering enterprises also remained small and supplied mainly local needs. As it developed into the most important colonial industry, lumbering depended on the presence of valuable timber and large streams. Whether large or small scale, the lumbering methods were much the same. Trees were felled with axes, stripped of branches, and cut into logs. Oxen hauled the logs on scoots, heavy sledlike vehicles, to a riverbank to be stacked in piles. When spring came the logs were floated downstream to a sawmill.

The earliest methods of cutting logs into planks were to split them with a tool called the froe or to saw them by a method called pit sawing. This sawing was frustrating. One man in a pit and another straddling the log worked with a vertical saw.

The first power-driven sawmill in America was established in 1633 on the Falls of Piscataqua between Maine and New Hampshire. This was many years before sawmills appeared in England. Sawmills multiplied quickly along streams that could be used both for power and transport, and laid a basis for a large lumber industry and a rapid advance in wood construction. Although windmills introduced by the Dutch were still common in 1776, the standard sawmill operated by water power. The saw was attached to one end of a wood beam that joined a crank on a water wheel. The log moved on a cogwheel-driven carriage (an American invention) against the saw. The wheels and the cogs were of wood, preferably hickory.

The early mills could saw more wood in an hour than ten men could saw in a day. Soon multiple saws, or gangsaws, were developed, some cutting 14 planks at a time. Towns frequently grew up around sawmills, vanguards of progress. Sawmills flourished throughout the country in 1776 and produced planks, clapboards, shingles, staves, and shipbuilding parts.

Lumbering for export concentrated in a few regions, especially New England with its abundance of waterpower and its stands of white pine excellent for shipmasts. The trees along the upper Hudson River provided New York with wood for housing and

Sawing logs into lumber with a pit saw—one man above the log, the other below—was a common practice in colonial days. (Courtesy Forest History Society, Santa Cruz, Calif.)

shipbuilding. Philadelphia got its timber supply from the Delaware valley, also a source of oak for shipmasts and spars. The pine forests of the Carolinas and Georgia were chiefly exploited for naval stores—pitch, tar, and turpentine. By 1776, however, the southern live oak had been found unsurpassed for shipbuilding, which caused lumbering to spread southward.

The leading lumbering region in 1776 was Maine, then a part of Massachusetts. Lumbermen in the 18th century possessed a rugged, and sometimes pugnacious, individualism. Their rough-and-ready way of life already was part of American folklore. Maine lumbermen so much resented the British Broad Arrow policy of marking trees with an arrow to reserve them for the Royal Navy, that timber may be included with "tea, taxes, and tyranny" as a cause of the American Revolution. The feudal principle of the Royal forest, successive Acts of Parliament, and exasperated British forest surveyors did not impress the New Englanders. Not appreciating having the best stands of white pine and oak set aside, they went right ahead and cut them in defiance of the law. Eventually, British attempts to enforce the law or to seize illegally cut timber were resisted with violence.

The first sea skirmish of the Revolution, called the Lexington of the Seas by James Fennimore Cooper, occurred off Machias, Maine, in May of 1775. The skirmish was over a shipment of pine lumber that townspeople prevented a British ship from commandeering. The ship was chased, captured, renamed *Liberty*, and decorated with evergreens. Since New England woodsmen already were fighting the British, they readily joined forces with the armed rebellion as it spread through the rest of the country.

The early resistance of the lumber regions cost the British their supply of masts. When the American shipments of masts ended in July 1775, the British neglected to revive their lapsed timber agreements with Sweden thinking the Revolutionary War would be over quickly. The Royal Navy, in a state of disrepair toward the end of the War, failed to give its usual good performance against the French. This prevented the Royal Navy from effectively supporting British troops.

Forest Products and Industries

In 1776 a number of important industries were closely related to lumbering: manufacture of naval stores, charcoal, and potash;

and the tanning industry. Naval stores include turpentine as well as pitch, tar, and resin. All were indispensable in shipyards for protecting surfaces and calking seams of wood ships. The naval industry spread all along the coast, but especially in the Carolinas and Georgia where southern pine, an ideal source, was prevalent and the harvesting season long. Workers chipped a flat surface on the trunks and drew off the amber-colored resin from which turpentine was distilled. Tar was produced by melting the resinous juices from deadened wood and further heated to make pitch. A single cord of longleaf pine produced 40 or 50 gallons of tar.

Charcoal became a versatile substance by 1776. It was the fuel used in iron making and in glassmaking; it was also used to make gunpowder, printers' ink, and black paint. Charcoal also served as a filter to purify liquids, as a deodorizer, and as insulation for ice storage. In the home the uses of charcoal were more surprising. It served as good toothpowder, and a small dose, swallowed, "settled the stomach."

Charcoal is produced by slowly burning wood with a restricted supply of air. This reduces the production of water and gases, leaving more or less pure carbon. In the 18th century the wood was burned in brick kilns or in earth-covered mounds with vents to control combustion. Constant attendance, for weeks at a time, was required to prevent explosion of gases.

The ashes of green sap-filled hardwoods provided potash and with further refinement a product called pearl ash. Both were needed as alkalis in the manufacture of soap and glass. The process was simple—the wood ash was boiled down into a thick brown salt. Thus, making potash became a common household or village industry. Ashes from burned trees provided a ready source of cash to the farmers clearing land. Ashes could either be gathered and sold to the manufacturer or made into potash in the family home.

The early family derived many other homemade products from their woodlot. Maple sugaring was a major activity in late winter in the North. Innumerable medicinal concoctions came from tree barks, roots, and leaves. Sassafras, long considered a sovereign remedy, had been one reason the English were eager to start productive colonies here. Sassafras leaves boiled made a spring tonic. Ground holly bark relieved ague; slippery elm helped sore throats. The twigs of black spruce, boiled and sweetened, made "spruce beer," rich in vitamin C, and so a cure for scurvy. Root beers and a tonic beer were made from birch sap.

Dyes were extracted from bark: deep brown from butternut, gold from tuliptree, yellow from birchbark oil which also was made into a perfume. Red oak bark yielded a furniture stain. Settlers could count on finding the honey and wax left by bees in hollow trees. A very large hollow beech tree or a walnut tree might contain 200 pounds of clear honey.

Tanning, a major industry, depended on a supply of tree bark. Animal hides were soaked in a lye made from wood ash to remove the hair, then placed in an astringent solution of tannic acid, or tannin, made from crushed oak or hemlock bark and water. The solution, absorbed by the hides, turned them into heavy, impermeable leather. Newly crushed bark would be added to the solution periodically, and the "spent" bark sold as fuel. The bark was provided by farmers or was a byproduct of lumbering. In some places tanbark mills ground the bark. The vats, barrels, and most of the tools and machinery used in tanning were of wood.

Almost all industries of the time depended on wood or wood products for fuel or supplies and tools. Printing was on small hand presses with working parts of iron, but the heavy frames were of wood. A cider press consisted of a wheel made of a thick oak plank that turned on a wood axle drawn by a horse. A carpenter's braces were of wood except for an inset of metal to hold the bit. Planes were of wood except for the blade. Gristmills, rag-carpet machines, corn shellers, boring engines, cotton balers, and spinning and weaving equipment were made almost wholly of wood. In the salt-boiling industry, which made salt out of seawater, it took a cord of wood to boil 11 bushels of salt out of the brine. From woodpiles to ball bearings (of close-grained hardwood), wood was an essential resource of 18th century industry.

Wood from Woodlots

The domestic life of early American farmers in 1776 clearly and richly exemplified an age of wood. Virtually every object on a farm and in a home was wholly or partly made of wood: house, barn, and outbuildings; fencing; vehicles; implements; tools; furniture; and utensils. To succeed farmers needed to be part-time lumbermen, carpenters, coopers, and woodcarvers. With the rapid growth in population, a farmer could obtain a steady income by chopping hardwood for charcoal kilns, firewood for villagers, and tunnel timbers for local mines. Timber was cut when families had no other chores on the farm. The winter's major occupation involved restocking the firewood supply and carving treen, the woodenware and implements a family used each day.

Many settlers may have been hostile to the forest before it had been cleared sufficiently for planting crops, but the wood from their woodlots brought a sensitive and discriminating appreciation. Wood was considered a substance with a soul. Stronger by weight than iron, wood was easily worked and was beautiful. Each piece possessed its own character. Yet wood was versatile enough to be adapted to the purposes of a craftsman. Had wood not been so common, transformation of it into a whole world of useful and beautiful objects might have seemed miraculous. Undoubtedly, colonial families felt for these objects, often made with their own hands, a sense of value and pride of possession that cannot be matched today with mass-produced goods.

A settler, like a lumberman, depended on an ax for cutting wood, and learned to use it with considerable dexterity. Early settlers found the European ax, almost unchanged since Roman times, too awkward to meet the challenge of American forests. By the 18th century, a new American ax had been developed. Heavier, with the handle set forward, it cut deeply and precisely with a graceful and balanced swing rather than a strenuous one. The long, thin handle was usually of ash or hickory. Every community had a craftsman who specialized in making ax handles; he designed them to have an individualized balance and feel that suited a particular owner. The American ax became a symbol of the free and resourceful frontier spirit.

Other axes and tools were available for working the felled timber: a pitching ax, a broadax, an adz (a hoe-shaped ax for trimming logs), a mortise ax, and a post ax. With these and a crosscut saw, maul, and wedges, settlers could undertake whatever construction was necessary. They could turn out their own shingles, planks, and staves, using a drawknife for tapering.

Log Cabins and Virginia Fences

Pioneers clearing a new farm would likely build first a log

cabin for the family home. Prominent as the log cabin is in American folklore, it was, in fact, imported from Europe. The Puritans in New England never lived in log cabins. At first they copied the Indians' U-shaped huts of bent saplings covered with thatch or bark. Sometimes they built over cavelike excavations in hillsides. But they quickly developed the New England saltbox, a wood-framed house with clapboard sheathing.

The standard log cabin, a traditional Scandinavian structure, was introduced by the Swedes on the Delaware River in 1638. It was not found elsewhere until after 1700, when Scotch-Irish immigrants began to copy it. Because log cabins were easily built and repaired, warm, dry, durable, and bullet-proof, they rapidly were adopted as the ideal structure for the frontier. Not only houses, but churches, schools, and other public buildings were made of logs.

An average log cabin required about 80 logs, as well as smaller timbers to form gables and shakes — usually of pine or cypress — for the roof. Packed dirt or puncheons, split logs flat-side up, made the floor. A ceiling of clapboards formed a sleeping loft; a notched log served as a ladder. The door might be a single plank from a large tree or made of clapboard with leather or hickory hinges. The chimney would be cat and clay — heavy sticks embedded in clay or mortar. A mixture of moss, clay, sticks, and straw filled gaps in the logs. If there were windows, they would be sliding boards or crossbars with greased paper. Wood pegs called treenails (pronounced "trunnels") held the roof structure together; the wall logs were notched. "Raising" a log cabin became a community project, with the four best axmen stationed at the corners to do the notching. In the isolation of the wilderness, the log cabin could be put up by a man and woman in a few days.

Furnishings were as simple as the house: a bedframe of poles attached to a wall, a split-slab table with legs set into the floor, three-legged stools that would not rock on the uneven surface, wood pins in the walls for hanging clothing.

After finishing the cabin, pioneers would construct in the same simple manner whatever outbuildings they needed: sheds, outhouse, barn, and smokehouse. Eventually a second story might be added to the cabin along with a clapboard exterior. A second cabin could have carefully squared logs and mortise-and-tenon

The log cabin was the ideal structure for the frontier, (Illustration by Gunard E. Hans, architect, Forest Prod. Lab.)

fastening to make it airtight and perhaps include amenities such as a staircase and room partitions. The new and the old cabins later could be connected with a covered passageway, called a dogtrot or breezeway, forming what was known as a two-pens-and-a-passage house.

A fireplace in a log cabin, as in larger houses in established settlements, was designed for logs 2 or 3 feet thick. The forests allowed Americans to enjoy bigger fires than those in European castles. The hearth was the center of family life: cooking, reading, sewing, whittling, conversation, and courtship. The fireplace, not an efficient way of heating a house, let most of the heat escape up the chimney. It could be very cold a few feet away from the hearth. However, the fireplace seemed to radiate a spiritual warmth and cheer just as it does today.

Settlers had local preferences in species and combinations of firewood. In Maine, for example, they liked hemlock with snow dumped on to keep it burning longer. In fall a family's woodpile would be as large as the cabin to provide them with from half to a full cord of wood a day in winter.

As farmers cleared their fields, they surrounded them with fences, another convenience Americans owed to their forests. In Europe, with wood rare, hedges and ditches made the more common boundaries. The most primitive fences, put up with a minimum of time and labor, provided barriers of branches and trunks or stumps with their roots turned up. More permanent fences included the Swedish post-and-rail fence — often of locust, a species extremely resistant to decay — and the Pennsylvania fence with cedar posts and chestnut rails.

The most common fence, other than the New England stone fence, was the Virginia rail fence, known also as snake fence or zigzag fence. Like the log cabin, the rail fence is characteristically American, although it originated in Scandinavia or, perhaps, Germany. Numerous advantages made this type of fence popular. It did not depend on posts placed in the ground, nor did it require nails, auger work, tying, or mortising. Fences could easily be torn down, moved, or repaired; the only requirement was a large amount of wood. The fence assembled by interlocking at an angle sets of 6 to 10 rails. At each angle, the stakes were crossed with a single heavy rail, called the rider, to hold them down. The zigzag fence averaged 7 or 8 feet in height, and required vast amounts of timber. About 26,500 rails were needed for every 4 miles of fence. The preferred species included locust, red cedar, chestnut, black walnut, and hickory. As long as the woods were abundantly available, the Virginia fence remained the most popular American fence.

Woods and Their Uses

Each species of wood has its own properties. The pioneer quickly learned to appreciate the shades of difference between the various species, finding for each its best use. For special purposes, he combined species. A rocking chair, for instance, might contain 10 or 15 species of wood, each with a specific property. Pegs would be made of a hard wood; soft woods cradled load, and springy woods carried weight. Rockers of black walnut would not creep forward as would those of maple or hickory made slick by wear.

A chair might be put together without nails or glue by inserting parts make of seasoned wood into parts made of green wood, which, while drying, would shrink and lock tight. Even a fishing rod made of three pieces was of different species: ash for the first joint, hickory for the second, and bamboo for the tip. Since properties of woods change with weather by warping and contracting or expanding, it was a fine art to match woods acting in opposite ways to keep joints tight. Treenails, used in this way, were more reliable than iron nails.

An expert on the distinctive properties and potentials of

different species of woods could be found on every farm. Thus, choice of a particular species of wood for a particular purpose was likely to prevail throughout the country, if the wood was available. Everyone knew, for instance, that in the absence of iron, blackgum (tupelo) wood made the best plowshares because its tortuous grain prevented splitting, and chestnut that resisted weather well made good fence rails but poor firewood because it would shower sparks when burning. This uniformity in choice of woods extended even to the whittled toys children made. In every colony bows and arrows were commonly of hemlock and whistles of chestnut or willow. But the uses of the more important woods were so numerous that each species is best considered separately.

Maple, because of its hardness, smoothness, and attractive color, became one of the most popular furniture woods and dominated household woodenware. Women presided over kitchens well-equipped with innumerable wood implements, gadgets, and machines that allowed the family to make bread, cheeses, cider, and other foods. Kitchen implements commonly made of maple included rolling pins, mashers, meat pounders, chopping boards, breadboards, pie crimpers, butter molds, boxes of all shapes, sizes, and purposes (tinder boxes, spice boxes, pillboxes), scoops, funnels, sieves, butter churns, and mortars and pestles for grinding grain, salt, and herbs. Among wood mechanical devices were apple parers and vegetable slicers (with metal blades), apple grinders for cider, cherry pitters, cheese presses and drainers, lemon squeezers, and sugar and flour sifters.

The settlers copied an Indian technique and hollowed out maple burls, knotlike growths with dense, tough, convoluted grain, to make durable and attractive bowls. Other tableware, such as trenchers, trays and platters, noggins, or pitchers, spoons and ladles, salt containers, eggcups, and tankards were often made of maple. Pails, piggins, tubs, washboards, clothespins, and buttons too, were made of maple. The shoe cobbler made his lasts of maple. Curly maple was used for musical instruments such as fiddles and dulcimers. Red maple was frequently selected for spinning wheels and tool handles. Maple was also valued as a firewood; its ashes could be used as a fertilizer and in soap-making.

Poplar was another wood often chosen for kitchenware. Soft, even textured, and easy to work, it has no taste or odor.

The art of making useful as well as beautiful baskets from wood splints survives in many rural areas. (Courtesy U. S. Forest Service)

Sometimes poplar was splinted to make baskets. A wood used more commonly for baskets was hickory, a tough, springy wood. Young trees, cut in winter when sap was not flowing, were well soaked and pounded before being cut into flexible splints for weaving into baskets.

Ash splints, strong and supple and easily peeled from small twigs, could also be woven into attractive baskets, as were "willow whips," thin, cordlike branches of green willow. Both hickory and ash were carved into basket hoops. Clothes hampers, cradles, market baskets, and similar indispensable containers of assorted shapes and sizes were made in this manner. Apart from basketry, hickory was used for tools, wagon wheels, furniture, and fences. Torches were made from hickory bark, and, of course, hickory provided the long-remembered "hickory stick" of the early schools. Ash, noted for its versatility, is white, hard, resilient, and durable. These qualities were valued by wheelwrights, cartwrights, and makers of furniture and tool handles. Coopers used ash for barrel and keg hoops; black ash and swamp ash were converted into hoop poles.

Beech, a heavy, hard, attractive wood unaffected by water, was usually reserved for household ware that received rough usage, such as rolling pins, meat pounders, and scoops. Chestnut, a lighter weight but also a very durable wood, was used for the same purposes, as well as for fencing and construction.

Oak could be relied on wherever great strength was needed; the proverbial "strong as an oak" testifies to its reputation. Oak with other woods, like hemlock and tupelo, was chosen by carpenters for floors of bridges, stables, and warehouses. In the home table boards and boxes were often oak, and in the well there was likely to be an oak bucket. White oak, the preferred wood for ship timbers and beams in dams and bridges, lasted although alternately wet and dry. It served well in wagon and coach frames, coach wheel spokes, harrow teeth, treenails, and whiphandles. White oak was selected for barrels and casks holding liquids; red oak, for flour and sugar barrels.

Pine served the most purposes with least difficulty of all of the woods in American forests. Common in all kinds of construction, pine was used in large quantities in bridges, ships, and houses. Inside a home pine made handsome flooring, ceilings, and paneling. In homes of the architecturally ambitious it was used for carved woodwork, shelves, and cupboards. Ordinary furniture was customarily made of pine. Pine was used in the grammar school for hornbooks, slabs that held lesson cards in place; a blackboard, a slab painted black; and benches. Powder horns, essential in a frontier household, were of pine.

The unsurpassed excellence of white pine for shipmasts gave it an importance in the War of Independence. Because it is soft and easily worked as well as strong, white pine was also much used for clapboards, chair seats, tubs, barrels, buckets, cheese and butter boxes, and knife trays, as well as other kitchen implements.

Pitch pine was known as candlewood because splinters from the wood made tapers for conveying flames from one fireplace to another. Its knots made torches for outdoor lighting, carried in iron cages held on a pole. Gathering pitch pine knots was a routine farm chore in the fall. Pine wood made good kindling, but was rarely used for fuel, because it burned too quickly and gave out sparks. Pine roots and branches were sometimes woven into baskets.

Several species of birch, a remarkably versatile wood, grew abundantly. Canoes were made from green bark of the white birch, which contains much oil and sheds water well. Homemade brooms consisted of slivers or twigs of birch tied to a birch handle. Branches were bent into hoops for barrels. Staves, pail handles, gunstocks, pegs, boxes, washboards, and clothespins were often made of birch. The beautiful brown heartwood of black and red birch, easily split and turned, was highly esteemed by furniture makers. The inner bark of white birch was sometimes used as writing paper in schools; ordinary paper, made from rags, was relatively expensive. In the north woods hunters fashioned horns for moosecalls from birchbark. The bark was also used to make boxes. Since yellow birch burns slowly and gives out great heat, it was used in bake ovens. Lye was obtained from its ashes for making soap and bleaching clothes.

Cedar, smooth, light, strong, and durable, was ideal for small boats and shingles and made good pails, firkins (butter dishes), churns, washtubs, and keelers (milktubs). Balladeers fashioned guitars out of cedar. Redcedar was frequently used for chests and other furniture, coffins, and barrels.

Black walnut was then, as now, an excellent wood for furniture. It was abundant enough to be used even for fencing, as well as for gunstocks and assorted objects of decorative qualities, such as musical instruments and checkerboards. Cherry, another valuable wood, made furniture of great beauty.

Carpenters and Coopers

Every craftsman in a village shop of 1776 had preferences in wood species. In a carriage shop, which turned out not only coaches and shays but also wagons, buckboards, and oxcarts, selection was ash, cherry, and poplar for the body of a carriage, and usually hickory or maple for wheels and running gear. The wood was seasoned by exposure to the sun and air for at least 2 years. Butternut wood, lightweight and durable, frequently was chosen for paneling in coaches. A wheelwright also used the smooth, tough wood of sycamore for wagon wheels and white elm, hickory, and gum wood that would not split for hubs. Spinning wheels and the smaller flax wheels with rims of very thin split wood were made of hardwoods.

Shuttles (frequently of persimmon wood), hand reels, hand looms, spools, and other wood implements used in spinning and weaving in a home or in shops were manufactured by a carpenter. Carpenters also produced pine and cedar shingles and clapboards, maple and pine four-post beds, chests and other furniture, tools and farm implements, and all of the smaller woodenware that was not ordinarily carved or put together in a home. Bowls, plates, and similar items were called turner's ware because they were made on a lathe.

Laurel wood, so often made into spoons in Pennsylvania, came to be known as spoonwood. Out of buckeye wood the carpenter gouged cradles and sugar troughs or sliced it into trays and trenchers. Dogwood was turned into mallets, vises, horse-collars and mill-wheel cogs; sycamore, aside from wheels, into windlasses and pulley blocks; and tuliptree wood, into boxes. The stringy inner bark of red and white elms was adopted for bedcords and chair bottoms. Water pipes and pumps were made from pine, hemlock, poplar, and especially baldcypress, virtually unaffected by water. Carpenters also undertook all varieties of construction, using in addition to oak, other woods such as hemlock, tupelo, yellow-poplar, and larch.

The importance of a cooper's shop has already been

suggested. Not only barrels indispensable for shipping and storage were turned out, but also other staved vessels, such as tubs, buckets, churns, and pipes. These smaller items were classified as "white cooperage" and made from pine, beech, maple, birch, and hickory. Basswood, instead of being cut into staves, was hollowed out to make casks, vats, and even beehives; it was also used for grain boxes and corn-grinding mortars.

Two kinds of barrels were used: "tight" or "wet," and "slack" or "dry." "Tight" barrels of white oak had to be watertight to hold wines, molasses, and other liquids. They required considerable skill. "Slack" barrels, used for grain and sugar, required less skill. They were made of a variety of woods: red, oak, maple, elm, ash, hickory, chestnut, and pine. A cooper and his apprentice could make two white oak "tight" barrels a day and four or five red oak "slack" ones.

Special shapes and kinds of wood needed to be found to suit specific purposes. A sapling that had grown curved around a log or rock could be carved into a scythe; twisted parts of large branches became parts for harnesses and ox yokes. Ox yokes were curved, with four holes for two oxbows, and locked with a wood key.

Ash or hickory, being strong and lightweight, was used for yokes. Pliable green walnut and red elm were used for bows; as they dried they hardened into permanent form. Forked sticks became pokes and yokes kept on the necks of barnyard animals to prevent them from escaping through fences. The sticks became divining rods, too. Saplings bent at the root were ideal for sled runners. Straight sticks made beanpoles and whipstocks.

Sections of hollow hemlock logs made feed boxes, troughs, and salt mortars. Sometimes slices of solid logs were used as cart wheels. Knots and burls of elm, ash, birch, chestnut, walnut, and maple were fashioned into cups and bowls; pieces of hornbeam, into hinges and latches. Hollowed blocks of wood made large wood shoes for humans and for horses to walk on swampy ground. Pieces of elm rind made natural chair seats and baskets. Certain kinds and shapes of wood could be assembled into traps for small and sometimes large animals; a forceps-shaped log trap was used for bears.

Every wood implement around the farm—which means virtually every implement—resulted from an ingenious and intricate collaboration with the shape and the quality of a piece of timber. This involved subtle and precise splitting, sawing, carving, or bending of wood into shovels, rakes, hayforks, flails, hoes, billhooks, ladders, plow moldboards, even wood spades and plowshares. But this, of course, could be said of every wood building, ship, piece of furniture. No wonder Thomas Jefferson at Monticello wrote in a letter, "I have thought myself obliged to decline every application which has been made me for timber of any kind, without that resource I could not have built as I have done, nor could I look forward with any comfort."[8]

The fine furniture of the 18th century illustrates the fact that wood articles could be not only well made but also of high artistic quality. In the small towns in 1776 a carpenter still made the furniture, but in cities furniture making was divided among a number of craftsmen: joiners, turners, cabinetmakers, chair-makers, upholsterers, and carvers. In a village carpenter shop the furniture produced remained as plain as it had been in the 17th century. There were strong, simple, straight-backed chairs; benches (forms and settles); stools of maple or other hardwoods; long, heavy oak tables; and four-post beds and built-into-a-corner "jack" beds. The chairs and benches were dignified, but not comfortable; they lacked upholstery, and people sat straight-backed. Furniture that could serve more than one purpose was preferred: chairs with backs that could be dropped to form tables and high-backed settles that could be converted into beds. In the course of the 18th century, however, the plain-style furniture had been replaced in towns and cities by the elegant styles of fashionable European furniture. Many of the cabinetmakers in cities had served their apprenticeships in England then immigrated to America.

American craftsmen faithfully copied English styles even while joining the movement for political independence. Nevertheless, a distinct American accent did develop within certain of the established styles. Characteristic American preferences, such as substituting native American woods like tuliptree, poplar, and cherry for the European woods emerged. Occasionally the early Americans were influenced by ethnic styles, such as the heavy Dutch furniture and the brightly painted furniture of the Pennsylvania Germans. Furthermore, each craftsman had his own ideas. Each piece had some characteristic deviation, a stylistic signature, to distinguish it from the work of other craftsmen. Subtle differences appeared in furniture according to the city in which a piece was made; each city, such as Boston, New York, Philadelphia, and Charleston, had its local preferences.

The prevailing wood for fine furniture was walnut, although maple was still frequently used, especially for parts subject to heavy wear or strain. Cherry, pine, and other woods also continued to be used. For both walnut and maple furniture, a painted finish became customary. After about 1750 mahogany, imported from the West Indies, began to a certain extent to replace walnut for fine cabinetwork.

Walnut lent itself to the graceful, curvilinear shaping characteristic of the Queen Anne style dominant in the early 18th century. This style was never surpassed for lightness, simple elegance, and integrated design. Its elongated S-curve motif emerged in the silhouette of all of its parts.

The Chippendale chair had straight rather than curved front legs, scroll and leaf carving, and Chinese ornamental touches. About 1776 new kinds of furniture gained acceptance, including the loveseat, chairs and couches with upholstered backs, side chairs, padded wing chairs, and the rocking chair. The creation of the rocking chair has sometimes been attributed to Benjamin Franklin who owned one. Actually its inventor is not known. Someone thought of putting rockers on an ordinary chair, which is how almost all rocking chairs were made until about 1800.

The most popular chair in America in 1776 was the Windsor chair. English in origin, it was lightweight, strong, and possessed simplicity that inspired native craftsmen to develop the style into more elegant forms than the original. The back of the chair was curved and made of slender spindles. The toprail usually extended into arms; sometimes the chair had a writing arm. In America the seat was often of pine and the spindled back of hickory, which being supple and strong, yielded comfortably to the back pressure of the sitter. The Windsor chair was the favorite chair of John Adams. For the porch at Mount Vernon, George Washington ordered 24 oval back chairs from Philadelphia, where the finest chairs in this style were made.

The dining table was a square dropleaf table. It had matching semicircular end tables that could be added to extend the table or they could be joined to form a separate serving table. For general purposes, there was a long "stretcher" table with drawers.

In 1776 coffee drinking was in a coffeehouse and tea drinking in a home around a delicate tea table. Folding card tables were a popular innovation. During the 18th century card playing had "caught on" in America, even among the descendants of New England Puritans.

During the 18th century a chest of drawers replaced the plain chest. A tall chest was called a highboy while a lower one, a dressing table with drawers, was called a lowboy. In New England these chests were elaborated by a blockfront cut with raised surfaces at each end and a recessed center. This design was an original American contribution to furniture style. The highboys and even larger pieces called double chests were massive—from 7 to 8 feet high—indicative of the large dimensions of the American room in 1776.

A piece of furniture that had become more sophisticated was the desk. Originally just a writing board, it became a slant-top desk, then a secretary desk which added a bookcase or cabinet to the writing desk. Often the desk had fine carving. Among the smaller pieces in the fashionable household were candlestands and a corner cupboard for porcelain and other valuable houseware. The cupboard sometimes was built into the paneling. Mirrors were large and decorated with carved walnut or mahogany frames. Beds were four-posters, often with carved ornaments, and were curtained.

In 1776 the impressive grandfather clock stood in the hall. The expensive clockcase and the works, too, were commonly made of wood. Often a family bought the works first and suspended them on a wall. When enough money was saved, the cabinetmaker came to the house and constructed a case. Most often it was made of walnut, although mahogany or pine served as common alternatives. The case was either plain or blockfronted and elaborately carved with scrolls and shell motifs. The cases made in 1776 in Pennsylvania and Newport, Rhode Island, were unsurpassed by the best European work of the time.

The most prominent craftsmen achieved a high level of art; their furniture was virtually flawless. John Cogswell of Boston became famous for his bombé, or kettle-shaped, furniture. In Newport the Goddards and Townsends formed a cabinetmakers' cooperative and created the first blockfronted furniture. Philadelphia possessed a strong furniture-making tradition. As early as 1722, 100 chairmakers and cabinetmakers were established there, and in 1776 they turned out Chippendale furniture of outstanding beauty, design, and richness of carving. Thomas Affleck and William Savery of Philadelphia and Gilbert Ash of New York were well known for their excellent Chippendale furniture.

Almost all of the leading furniture craftsmen contributed their skills to the cause of American independence; several made especially memorable contributions. Upon arrival in Philadelphia as a delegate to the Continental Congress, Thomas Jefferson stayed with Benjamin Randolph, an eminent cabinetmaker. Jefferson showed Randolph a design for a small portable desk. Randolph made the desk, and in the summer of 1776 Jefferson composed the Declaration of Independence on it. Randolph served as an officer in the Philadelphia City Troop and was with Washington when he crossed the Delaware in December of the same year.

Philadelphia cabinetmaker Francis Trumble was honored by receiving two orders to supply Windsor chairs and other furniture for Independence Hall. British soldiers stationed there during the British occupation of Philadelphia kept warm by burning all of Trumble's original furniture! Quaker David Evans of Philadelphia, forbidden by his religion to bear arms, produced tentpoles, camp chairs, and cots for use in the field.

American Architecture

Like furniture, American architecture developed from crude but sturdy beginnings to high levels of sophistication and artistic refinement. In New England the first permanent dwellings built by the Puritans were modeled on the old English timber-frame house with wattle and daub or brick infill between the exposed framing members. An overhanging second story was frequently used simply because this was the common style in English towns. The wattle and daub construction did not provide sufficient insulation against the cold New England winter. Exteriors were soon sheathed with oak or pine clapboards, the brick excluded, and the wood frame improved to withstand the abrupt changes of climate. This resulted in the characteristic New England saltbox, practical and unpretentious, and still the prevailing style of house in 1776.

In cities clapboards might be painted, but in small towns and in the countryside they were left natural to weather. Painting, considered somewhat ostentatious, was not customary until the 19th century. On the interior pine paneling and wide, sometimes doubled, floorboards provided further protection against the cold. A house was most likely to be rectangular, with a fireplace at one end. Cypress shingles usually covered the roof.

The first architects of the saltbox houses were master carpenters who, like the cabinetmakers, had served apprenticeships in England. In 1776 local carpenters still designed and built ordinary houses. A carpenter made up for a lack in materials by using skill and imagination. Houses always had individual character while conforming to the general style.

In the Middle States and the South, although wood houses were common, the preferred building materials were brick and stone. The Dutch in New York decorated the interiors of their houses with woodwork elaborately carved with considerable originality and frequently painted white. For the hot summers, they invented a traditional feature of American houses, the front porch. Meanwhile the veranda with columns was becoming customary on plantation houses in the South. The German settlers in Pennsylvania built a kind of log house that was more permanent and required more painstaking labor than the standard log cabin. Made of carefully squared, precisely placed timbers, it had a second story that usually rested on wood columns, often richly carved.

In the West in 1776 beyond the frontier, several unrelated traditional styles of architecture made use of wood. Indian tribes of the eastern and northwestern coastal forests skillfully erected buildings of wood; they also made their canoes, sleds, weapons, and implements of wood. In the East the Indians built huts, wigwams, and long community houses that incorporated frameworks of poles covered with birch or elm bark, and they built log palisades to protect villages. Even on the Great Plains and in the western mountains, some tribes acquired timber and made strong permanent dwellings of log frames covered with earth. In the forests of gigantic redwood, cedar, fir, and spruce of the northern Pacific coast, Indians had an economy and culture based on wood. They used wood for totem poles, and their houses with gabled roofs were skillfully and firmly constructed out of planks of split cedar or redwood and decorated with carvings.

The French settlers in the Mississippi Valley had the palisade house with vertical logs set in the ground or in a foundation. In New Orleans wood buildings, although less common than those of stone and brick, had galleries and outside staircases and were raised on a high foundation as a precaution against floods.

The Spanish in the Southwest chose adobe for their missions and forts. Wood, however, was used for the heavy roof beams, doors, window frames, simple furniture, and the gallery, a covered walk which was of heavy carved beams and brackets resting on round wood columns. In 1776 the Spanish were extending their missions and outposts northward in California. Russians explored southward from Alaska, building log houses, forts, and churches.

Although the use of brick and stone increased in the colonies during the 18th century, wood in 1776 remained the principal building material and far surpassed its rivals in range and versatility. This fact startled most of the Europeans drawn to America by the War. They had forgotten how recently in their history wood construction had been common in their cities. After closer observation, their initial perplexity frequently gave way to expressions of admiration. Boston is described in a passage from a travel diary of the Abbé Robin, chaplain of the French army during the War:

> The construction of the houses is surprising to European eyes. They are entirely of wood, not built in the heavy and somber fashion of our ancient towns, but regularly and well-lighted. The carpenter-work is neat and well done, and the outsides are of thin and smooth planks, overlapping like the tiles of our roofs; they are painted gray, adding greatly to the pleasing appearance. The roofs are ornamented with balustrades, doubtless because of fires; the foundations consist of a wall about a foot high—one sees at a glance how much healthier these houses must be than ours.[9]

By 1776 American architecture in wood had approached the level of the most accomplished European architecture. As in Europe, the best 18th-century American architecture was due to architects collaborating with skilled artisans. Architecture became part of a gentleman's education. An architect was ordinarily an amateur engaged in some other profession, as was Andrew Hamilton, a lawyer, who designed Independence Hall; George Washington, who contributed to the design of several buildings; or Thomas Jefferson, who was one of the finest architects of that period. At the same time, however, master carpenters who specialized in building fine houses had achieved a wide knowledge of their subject and, with it, something close to professional status.

Both architects and master carpenters usually worked without blueprints. They made sketches as construction progressed, and consulted the architectural handbooks, mostly English, which set forth the stylistic conventions of the period. Georgian was the conventional style, popularly known today as Colonial. Its stately, symmetrical forms, which produced the most popular style of domestic architecture in U.S. history, were derived from classical and Renaissance sources, and were formulated early in the century. By 1776 the style was beginning to develop into a new, more direct imitation of classicism called Classical Revival, of which Jefferson's designs were the first great American examples.

The only major difference between English and American Georgian was American Georgian houses were often built of wood, especially in New England, where the tradition of wood construction was strongest. Because stone was the conventional material depicted in style handbooks, the wood was sometimes grooved, beveled, and painted and sanded to resemble cut stone. One of the finest examples is the Lee Mansion in Marblehead, Massachusetts, erected in 1768. The most famous American house of the time, Washington's Mount Vernon, has exterior walls of planks of longleaf pine, beveled and painted with a sand finish to imitate stone masonry.

Even in American brick and stone Georgian houses, however, the elaborate door and window enframements were customarily of carved wood. Sometimes the entire front was of wood, with brick gable ends, which allowed greater freedom to embellish the front windows and door with carving. Oddly enough, the entirely wood Georgian houses of New England were plain and had very little carved decoration on the exterior; this was perhaps due to a lingering puritanical prejudice against any display of luxury.

The wood trim on the exterior of a Georgian house was usually painted white. The doorways were made especially impressive by elaborate carving. Flanking a paneled double door there would be pilasters surmounted by intricately carved panels, or capitals, which supported the entablature, the triangular or arch-shaped projection over the door. There might be similar entablatures above windows. The carving above a door was often topped by a carved pineapple, a symbol of hospitality. On the roof, flatter than those of earlier houses, was a balustrade, or captain's walk, a fenced enclosure painted white.

All Georgian houses had rich woodwork in interiors. In early houses, entire rooms were wood paneled. After 1750 wallpaper and hangings began to replace some of the paneling, although the Lee house in Marblehead has a room that is paneled with mahogany. Above the fireplace in the Lee house is an elaborate panel with delicately carved pendants of flowers, fruits, and leaves; on either side are pilasters, capitals, and other precisely rendered classical motifs. Most fireplaces in Georgian homes offered similar displays of a woodcarver's art.

The thick walls of a house created deep window recesses, which were faced with paneling hinged near the windows to form shutters. Staircases were wide and imposing; ends of steps were exposed and carved; balustrades were turned and often carved. In the Graeme Park Mansion in Horsham, Pennsylvania, a good example of Georgian stone construction, stairs and banisters are of heavy white oak, and the remaining woodwork is of yellow pine. Woodwork was customarily painted in one flat color, such as strong gray-blue, dark red, or olive-green, rather than the white or pastels that today are associated with colonial interiors.

The detached, or freestanding, house had become the standard American dwelling, a reflection of American individualism made possible by the ready availability of construction materials, especially wood.

Churches, frequently made of wood, followed the pattern of domestic architecture, developing from a plain to an ornate style. A typical early church is the Old Meeting House in Hingham, Massachusetts, built in 1680, and said to have been constructed by ships' carpenters. A square, with plain clapboard walls, it has a balustrade and a small pointed spire. During the 18th century churches adopted the dignified classical detail and other carved

The Parson Capen House, its characteristic architecture brought to the New World by the early settlers, still stands in Topfield, Massachusetts. This house had been in use for 93 years at the time of the signing of the Declaration of Independence. (Courtesy Gunard E. Hans, architect, Forest Prod. Lab.)

The versatile Conestoga wagon assumed a legendary role in American history. This wagon, pulled by a six-horse team, was once used for carrying freight on the National Pike. (Courtesy Library of Congress)

decoration of the Georgian style, and added tall, graceful spires or bell towers that were almost always wood. Paneling and woodwork of the interiors were more austere than in Georgian homes but executed with equal skill. The galleries might be supported by pillars finely carved into the classical orders. A wood canopy was often placed above the carved wood pulpit as a sounding board. Pews were high backed. Woodwork both inside and out was commonly painted white.

The finest public building of the time is also the most famous — Independence Hall, the Old State House, in Philadelphia. It is an excellent example of Georgian in the brick-and-wood combination. The white wood superstructure for the clock contrasts with the deep red brick of the tower. A wood balustrade painted white adds grace and lightness. The roof was originally covered with cedar shingles made from submerged logs of New Jersey's cedar swamps. Interior woodwork is particularly ornate, executed in a bold and masterly fashion. Designs include fluted pillars and pilasters with richly carved Roman capitals, intricate egg-and-dart and leaf designs, elaborately wrought brackets under the treads of the stairs, and impressive pediments above doors and mantels. Independence Hall also provides an example of how American architecture already reflected social and political conditions different from those of Europe. Its plan, although modeled after English palaces, was adjusted to accommodate large democratic assembly rooms rather than the small audience chambers appropriate for royalty.

Wood Vehicles

Travel in 1776 was slow and without much comfort. Several kinds of vehicles were commonly used: small coaches; a shay or sedan chair, an original American two-wheeled vehicle that could seat two and had its carriage suspended on hickory springs; a gig, a light, open one-seat conveyance drawn by one horse. But these were mostly confined to cities, since roads between cities were generally very poor. In winter in the North, sleighs provided a smooth ride. A slow and jolting ride was available between major cities by stagecoach, which in good weather took 2 days for the 90 miles between New York and Philadelphia. The fastest and most comfortable means of overland travel was still by horseback.

For farmers and freight carriers the most simple vehicle was a cart, with two solid wood wheels attached to a wood axle; the diameters of the wheels equaled a person's height. The wheels, made very wide, would not easily sink in mud. There was also a flat wagon, but this was improved on early in the 18th century. German settlers in the Conestoga Valley of Pennsylvania developed the Conestoga wagon, which assumed a legendary role in the settlement of the American West.

The Conestoga was based on covered wagons of Europe, but given an emphatic downward curve toward the middle, so that the load would settle toward the center while traveling over the Pennsylvania hills. The front and rear panels, often decoratively carved, slanted downward and inward; wood bows were arched above the wagon bed; over these a tentlike covering was drawn. The wagon, usually made of oak and poplar, weighed more than 3,000 pounds and could carry 2 to 4 tons of goods. The largest wagons were drawn by eight horses. Conestoga wagons became the standard freight carriers in Pennsylvania. During Washington's winter at Valley Forge, Conestogas carried the army supplies.

Roads, Bridges, and Boats

The first American roads were muddy trails marked by blazed trees. Cluttered with fallen trees, stumps, and rocks, they were rough going for vehicles. An attempted improvement over muddy swampy passages was a pavement of small logs or saplings laid across the road; later this "pavement" was called a corduroy road. This expedient prevented coaches from sinking in the mud, but the logs, bumpy and slippery, had no solid foundation. The logs dipped or twisted loose and eventually split and rotted. When kept in good condition, these roads impressed European visitors who had seen nothing like them in their own countries, where roads were also generally bad. A French traveler wrote,

> Part of the road from New York to Newark runs through marshes. I found this section truly astounding . . . Built wholly of wood, with so much toil and preserverance, in the midst of water and shifting ground, this road proves what can be accomplished by the patience of men determined to conquer nature.[10]

British wood sailing ships disembark infantry and supplies in Boston Harbor in 1768. Engraving by Paul Revere, 1770. By 1775 one-third of the ships in the British Merchant Marine had been built in American shipyards. (Courtesy I.N. Phelps Stokes Collection, Prints Division, The New York Public Library, Astor, Lenox and Tilden Foundations)

A VIEW OF PART OF THE TOWN OF

Beaver   5 Mermaid   On friday Septr 30th 1768, the Ships of
Senegal   6 Romney   a Spring on their Cables, as for a regu
                           and Train of Artillery with two heav

The crude wood bridge arched the flood at Concord, Massachusetts, where embattled farmers fired the shot heard 'round the world on April 19, 1775. Plate III of Amos Doolittle's views of the battles of Lexington and Concord. (Courtesy Bancroft Collection, Prints Division, The New York Public Library, Astor, Lenox and Tilden Foundations)

TON IN NEW ENGLAND AND BRITTISH SHIPS OF WAR LANDING THEIR TROOPS. 1768

Even when roads were passable, a general lack of bridges presented obstacles to the traveler. Bridge building had just begun to advance beyond the use of a "raccoon bridge," a tree felled across a creek, or of a few logs tied together. Crude rafts were used for large streams. Most bridges were constructed of rough logs laid across beams, without any safeguards on the sides. On large rivers there were usually flatboat ferries, sometimes drawn across with the aid of pulleys. Occasionally, however, permanent bridges were built across major streams. A timber crib filled with stone would be built in midstream, and stone packed around the crib to prevent undermining; planks would be extended from the crib to the banks. On large streams the number of supports and sections was increased.

In 1761 Major Samuel Sewall achieved some technical advances in a wood bridge he built across the York River in Maine. The bridge, 270 feet long, had 13 sections. The center bridge section operated as a drawbridge. Each section was supported by four pilings of saplings driven into the river bottom by a pile-driving device. A large oak beam raised by pulleys and then released provided sufficient force to drive the supports into the mud.

The principles of the arch and truss, only beginning to be understood, were next introduced to bridge building. In 1764 a bridge, 120 feet long and 28 feet above the water, was built over the Shetucket River in Connecticut. This probably was the first use of trusses in American bridge building. The wood trusswork formed triangular patterns that gave the structure the nickname of "geometry bridge."

Travel on rivers was usually easier than over them. The early settlers adopted the Indians' light birchbark canoe for streams with rapids; the canoe could shoot the rapids in one direction and be carried around them in the other. Bark was lashed to a cedar frame with spruce roots and calked with balsam resin and pine pitch. The settlers also adopted the Indian practice of converting hollow sycamore trunks into dugout canoes, and for rocky streams they developed their own small, strong boat, the bateau.

The settlers eventually devised an improvement on the birchbark canoe by hollowing out white pine or tuliptree logs into canoes. These log canoes were still light enough to be portaged but stronger than the birchbark canoes. Sharpened ends made them faster and easier to maneuver. Canoes of this type carried pioneers up the eastern streams into the wilderness, then westward down the rivers beyond the Appalachians.

About 1750 on a western river, Jacob Yoder launched a boxlike craft he called a flatboat to carry river cargo. He built a low cabin onto a flat bottom of thick hardwood timbers and planking. Long keel boats with masts and sails, rafts, and barges also carried cargo down the rivers. On western rivers the flatboat was the primary cargo vessel until the arrival of the steamboat. Flatboats, from 10 to 20 feet wide and 20 to 60 feet long, required a crew of five or six. Driven by the current and guided by one or more long sweeps, flatboats carried grain, flour, furs, and settlers and their belongings. When the boats reached their destination downstream, they were broken up and sold for lumber.

Art of Shipbuilding

A French scholar who visited this country during the War of Independence wrote, "The art of constructing vessels has made more rapid progress in America than anywhere else."[11] In the 100 years prior to the Revolution, American shipbuilding had advanced from a small, scattered, part-time enterprise, which produced vessels mainly for fishing and coastal trade, to a major industry, which supplied a large domestic merchant fleet as well as foreign maritime interests. In 1775 one-third of the ships in the British merchant marine had been built in American shipyards.

Shipbuilding attracted skilled English and Dutch artisans, and at its best equaled the technical excellence of European shipwrights. With demand increasing both at home and abroad, American shipbuilders sold their ships as fast as they could make them. They had an advantage over their European rivals—a rich and steady supply of timber that made American ships the least expensive available.

Shipbuilding at first concentrated in New England with its large fishing and merchant fleets, excellent supply of ship timbers, and advanced lumbering industry. Boston, Newport, Portsmouth, and other New England towns continued to dominate the industry and launched half of all American tonnage in the years before the Revolution. The rapid expansion of shipbuilding during these years caused a geographical expansion of the industry. Philadephia and Baltimore became important building centers; ships were even built in inland cities like Reading, Pennsylvania, and sent downstream to the sea. In the southern states shipyards were well established by 1776; the ships they produced, although fewer in number than those of the North, surpassed northern ships in design and quality.

The outbreak of war in 1776, by interfering with trade and closing off the English and other foreign markets, dealt a serious blow to the shipyards. But the losses were made up to some extent by producing privateers to prey on British trade, sometimes very profitably, and by being commissioned by Congress to build a Continental Navy. Frigates were built for the war effort throughout the states.

Before the War American shipbuilders had been turning out ships of all kinds, although on the average they were smaller than European ships. The most prevalent kind was the schooner, an American innovation developed in New England early in the 18th century. A small ship with a narrow, sharp hull, it rode the surface of the water with speed and maneuverability.

Shipwrights, like other craftsmen, had to have a thorough knowledge of the properties and performance of different woods. Their range of choice was narrow, since few species met the qualifications for the principal parts of ships. Of the more than 500 species of trees in North America, only about 20 were ever used extensively in shipbuilding. The main qualifications for a species of wood for shipbuilding were great strength, hardness to withstand frequent blows or groundings, resistance to warping to minimize leaks, lightness to insure speed and carrying capacity, resistance to decay to insure durability, and tenacity to hold fastenings. Few species met all of these criteria. Some that did were inaccessible, too small, or of limited quantity. Only the largest, full-grown trees could be used for keels, sternposts, stems, frames, and spars. This meant virgin timber had to be used. Furthermore, naturally curved and bent timbers had to be found for certain parts of a hull. Shipbuilders usually stocked little of this timber. When orders arrived or a need arose, they went to a woods and selected the required pieces. Sometimes a shipwright owned a forest and selected suitable timber during the winter.

Decay, which occurs in warm, moist conditions, was the mortal enemy of wood ships. American shipbuilders used methods of cutting that reduced the risk of decay. The abundance of large trees allowed them to cut away the less resistant outer sapwood and to use only the durable heartwood. The timber they cut was in close proximity and could be stored outdoors, whereas timber shipped over long distances in closed storage tended to deteriorate.

The primary species of wood used in frames of American ships were white oak and live oak. Locust, also excellent, was not available in sufficient quantity and size. It was used mainly in top timbers and other small parts of a frame. White oak, the traditional wood for ship frames and the most abundant, was the usual choice. Tough and resilient, white oak could withstand very successfully the impact of grounding or of gunfire. Properly seasoned, it resisted decay, and its tannic acid content, although it might corrode ironwork, discouraged worms. Also, oak trees offered many large curved pieces for the shaped parts of the hull.

Live oak, a short, thick tree, is a fine-grained, heavy, durable wood. If seasoned, this wood made an almost indestructible ship frame believed to last 100 years. Like white oak, live oak offered many good curved pieces but was relatively heavy and difficult to work. Its use was limited to southern shipyards; later, live oak became the principal frame timber of the U.S. Navy.

Another timber used extensively in frames was the heartwood of chestnut. This tree grew large with wood lightweight and sufficiently durable if well seasoned. Redcedar, also lightweight and durable, was sometimes employed, but a lack of size and strength and insufficient quantities prevented it from becoming a major ship timber. Ash, strong and elastic, was often chosen for top timbers. In New England, especially in Maine, maple, beech, birch, hackmatack (tamarack), and spruce were used for ship frames, but because all were inferior to white oak, they were confined to small ships.

Two kinds of planking were used in wood ships. For the bottom and sides of the hull, builders required wood that was strong, easy to bend, resistant to decay, and able to withstand alternating heat, cold, water, and hot sun. These requirements were best met by white oak and southern pine. In this period white oak was the dominant wood for planking and also for the ceiling of the hold. For decks white pine was most often chosen because of its lightness and resistance to sun and weather. It was also

This figurehead of the goddess Galatea adorned the ship Galatea built in Charlestown, Massachusetts, in 1854 at the peak of the American clipper era. (Courtesy Mariners Museum of Newport News, Va.)

commonly selected for deckhouses and cabins, although in the finest ships teak and mahogany might be used.

White pine, one of the most satisfactory mast timbers in the world, reached heights of 150 feet with diameters of 3 feet or more. Qualities of strength, light weight, durability, and suppleness enabled it to bend in squalls without breaking. For small spars, spruce timber was occasionally used instead of white pine.

As in Europe, American ships were sometimes built according to carefully drawn drafts and specifications; small ships might be put together by eye and rule of thumb. The most common procedure was to use a model skillfully and precisely carved out of white pine and dark redcedar at a scale of 1/4 inch to a foot. Thus there would be a 25-inch scale model for a 100-foot vessel. The carving of the model was a delicate task. Since few scientific principles were established, a builder relied on his own judgment and taste.

The first step in putting together a ship was to lay a huge keel at a proper slope on keel blocks. The ship's carpenter then raised stem and sternpost in position onto the keel, and placed and bolted the floor timbers. Thus the bottom of the ship was outlined. The most difficult operation was raising the half-frames into position by a derrick, after which keelson, clamps, knees, and beams could be added. The final steps were planking, calking, and smoothing.

Treenails of locust and hickory steeped in tar were used throughout the ship; after they swelled in place with the aid of the tar, they held tight. Masts and spars were put in place after the ship was launched. Launching was always a festive occasion; a young woman or a carpenter riding the bowsprit christened the ship.

Art Forms of Wood

Projecting from a bow of a ship would be a realistically carved, brightly painted, wood figurehead. Each ship had a particular personality expressed by her name and figurehead. The crew associated the figurehead with the luck of the ship; the gallant, steadfast human figure, enduring storms and long voyages, must have commanded loyalty and reverence. Some imposing American figureheads that fell into the hands of the South Sea Islanders were worshiped as idols.

Until the middle of the 18th century, English and colonial ships featured carved lions, then seahorses and other animals. These were soon followed by allegorical and individual human figures. By 1776 American ships displayed carved portraits of Washington, John Hancock, and other patriots; portraits of a shipowner, his wife, or daughter; eagles; Indians; and personifications of liberty.

American shipcarvers favored soft pine for figureheads rather than the elm or oak customarily used in Europe. They worked from sketches and live models and carved from a single block. Carvers developed a native style that was spare and vigorous and emphasized the broad contours of a silhouette. American carvers preferred full-length, individualized portraits to the ornate three-quarter figures of European carvers. The figurehead leaned out from an elaborately carved scroll. Similar decorations were found throughout the ship; even cannon portholes were surrounded by carved wreathes.

Shipcarvers also produced wood decorative sculpture for homes and gardens, including architectural ornamentation, weathervanes, and decorative carving in relief on mantlepieces. William Rush, an outstanding shipcarver, carved a wood statue of Washington for Independence Hall. Woodcarvers turned out portraits, classical figures, busts of poets, and animal sculpture that are fine examples of American folk art. In the Southwest Spanish-Indian woodcarvers were creating religious sculpture in a distinctive style that fused Spanish Baroque with Indian geometric simplicity.

Signs with images carved in wood or painted on wood slabs advertised village shops. Wooden Indians were appearing in front of tobacco stores. A carving of a sailor identified the ship chandler's shop in seaport towns. Large wood watches, boots, and horseshoes announced a shopkeeper's wares to passers-by. Even public buildings were often represented by appropriate figures — a female personification of justice in front of a courthouse, a manacled man in front of a jail. Names of taverns or inns might be illustrated by a wood sign with a painting of a Turk's head, St. George and the dragon, or a Bacchus with grapes.

Several of the most famous early American painters, such as Benjamin West, Gilbert Stuart, Charles Willson Peale, and Matthew Pratt, began their careers by painting shop signs. Even

The boldly imaginative totem poles of the Northwest Coastal Indian Tribes served as memorials or for decorative purposes. Totem poles shown are located in Saxman Park, Ketchican, Alaska. (Courtesy U.S. Forest Service)

when artists turned to more ambitious subjects, they might continue to paint on wood, often used instead of canvas. Many itinerant portrait painters carried stacks of wood panels with them instead of canvas and stretchers. Connoisseurs of wood, they knew the woods least likely to warp, crack, or react to moisture.

Many artifacts indicate professional woodcarvers must have been fairly numerous in 1776. Amateur woodcarvers, however, who worked with a jackknife, were found everywhere. The jackknife became a Yankee trademark. Sailors, lumberjacks, farmers, and children expressed their creative impulses by whittling carved ships, chains, animals, and all kinds of household woodenware. Boys and girls created their own toys — whistles from willow branches, bows and arrows from hemlock, popguns from alder, and wood tops, hoops, and balls from white pine. John Adams remembered as a boy carving his own toy water wheels and windmills. Some professionals carved wood dolls, blocks, rocking horses, billiard balls, and chess sets.

Amateur carving could reach a highly accomplished level of art, as in the exquisite butter molds, boxes, cookie boards, and other woodenware carved with flower and geometric designs by the Pennsylvania Germans. Carving of wood decoys was another fine art and was adopted from the American Indians. A decoy had to be accurate in every detail. Not only ducks but all species of waterfowl sought by hunters were skillfully carved of wood.

Indian woodcarvings are also important examples of folk art, particularly the totem poles of the Northwest coastal tribes. The totem pole was a cedar column carved with boldly imaginative and intricate figures and designs, brightly painted. These poles ranged from 10 to 70 feet in height and from 1 to 3 feet in diameter and served as memorials or as decorative poles at the front of houses.

Appreciation of Wood

In retrospect life in early America was not only made possible, but it was made beautiful by wood. Appropriately Americans of that time chose the tree as a symbol of their country and its newly won liberty. Americans, at first, may have felt hostility toward the forest as an immediate obstacle to their plans and purposes. When they became settled, however, it did not take them long to realize how dependent they were on the forest. They became aware of the infinite variety of and indispensable uses of forest products in their daily lives. Their hostility then gave way to reverence for the tree as a symbol of the American way of life.

A series of "Tree" coins, minted in Massachusetts beginning in 1652, became the standard coinage for the early colonists. These coins consisted of sterling silver disks with detailed willow, oak, and later pine trees that were not easily counterfeited. Joseph Jenks, a colonial coin designer, perceptively asked, "What better thing than a tree to portray the wealth of our country?"[12]

Many of the Colonies placed the emblem of a tree on their flags. Later, a pine tree was portrayed on both the official seal and the flag of the state of Maine. American soldiers at the Battle of Bunker Hill fought under a flag that had a pine tree in one corner, and the first American naval cruisers flew a flag that bore a green pine tree in a field of white.

In many towns the meetings at which Americans made the decisions that led to the Revolution were held under venerable trees that became known as Liberty Trees. For a Liberty Tree in Providence, Rhode Island, the following dedication was written:

> We do, therefore, dedicate and solemnly devote this tree to be a Tree of Liberty. May all our councils and deliberations under its branches be guided by wisdom and directed to the support and maintenance of that liberty which our renowned forefathers sought out and found under trees and in the wilderness.[13]

PART 2

WOOD
IN THE
GROWING
NATION

The magnificent stands of white pine in the Lake States were harvested in a relatively short period of time to meet the building needs of mid-west cities and the settlers on the Great Plains. (Courtesy State Historical Society of Wisconsin)

1876

One hundred years after its founding the United States had become a continental nation of 45 million people. Having survived a civil war, the nation was now in the process of rapid industrial and urban expansion. The technological advances of the Industrial Revolution, which included the railroad, the telegraph, and the factory system, transformed the material and social life. As a result, Americans gradually moved from the country to the city. By the 1870s more than 20 percent of the population lived in cities; the largest city, New York, had a population of 1 million. The major cities provided a crowded refuge for most of the new European immigrants, arriving in increasingly vast numbers. Almost 3 million arrived in the 1870s; more than 5 million in the next decade.

In the centennial year of 1876 Colorado was admitted to the Union as the 38th state; the remaining of the present states, except for Hawaii, existed as territories. The frontier pushed westward with the advances of cattlemen, miners, and the first farmers of the Great Plains. The last of the independent Indian tribes were retreating.

In 1876 the National League of baseball teams was founded, and Mark Twain published *Tom Sawyer*. This was a time of economic depression and political scandal. The effects of the Panic of 1873 were widespread: business failures, high unemployment, and multiplying labor strikes. President Ulysses S. Grant, in his last year of office, apologized to Congress for the scandals that had caused several members of his cabinet to resign. In the November presidential election, a small margin of victory won by the Democratic candidate Samuel Tilden was disputed. Not until the next year was his Republican opponent, Rutherford B. Hayes, declared winner. Despite these troubles, a Centennial Exposition in Philadelphia was successful. The first American world's fair, the Exposition had displays of new inventions including the typewriter, the Corliss engine, and Alexander Graham Bell's first telephone.

The technological revolution and the rapid growth of population had a major impact on the forests. Railroads, telegraph lines, charcoal steel mills, and other industries consumed immense quantities of wood. The settlers on the treeless plains needed supplies of lumber for houses, fences, and construction purposes, since they had no woodlots or local sawmills.

New cities of the Midwest, such as Chicago, Cleveland, and Indianapolis, were being built mostly of wood, while the expanding older cities in the East could not depend on their almost depleted local forests to meet their increasing requirements. The Civil War had made heavy demands on forest resources for fuel, fortifications, and supplies; one gun factory alone used 28,000 walnut trees for gunstocks. During the latter half of the 19th century, the value of forest products harvested each year rose from $60 million to almost $600 million.

By 1876 the largest lumbering operations had shifted from the East to the white pine forests of the Great Lakes region, close to the lucrative markets being opened by the railroads on the Great Plains. Lumbering was a fiercely competitive and highly speculative business dependent on quick profits. This encouraged careless and extravagantly wasteful methods of lumbering. An observer writing in 1870 complained that "the waste of lumber in the United States was almost criminal."[1]

On the Pacific coast where lumbering was just beginning, more than half of the timber felled was left to decay. The debris after lumbering operations fueled enormous forest fires that killed the young and secondary growth. Every summer major fires burned throughout the country. Some regions burned over and over again and reduced areas to desolate wasteland. Fires probably consumed as much of the virgin forests as lumbermen

Lumber jacks spend a rare moment of leisure. (Courtesy State Historical Society of Wisconsin)

cut. The worst fire of the time was also the worst natural disaster in American history. About 1,200 people were killed in the Peshtigo, Wisconsin, area on the night of October 8, 1871, when two million acres of virgin white pine were reduced to ashes. This was also the night of the great Chicago fire.

Most of the forest fires started by sparks from locomotives or by negligence. Some, however, were deliberately set by lumbermen or settlers to erase evidence of thefts of timber from government lands. Helping oneself to government timber was an American tradition from colonial days. The Federal Government lacked the power and necessary agents to prevent thefts. When federal agents did try to enforce the law, they encountered hostility and juries that refused to convict.

Both lumbermen and settlers saw no reason for the government to deny them the timber; to them it was obvious that the American forests were inexhaustible. For the government to withhold acres of timber that might be put to good use made no sense to them. In 1852 Representative B. C. Eastman of Wisconsin asserted that the lake country possessed "interminable forests of pine, sufficient to supply all the wants of the citizens in the country, from which this supply can be drawn for all time to come."[2] In 1876 the belief of the inexhaustibility of forests still prevailed not only in the lake country, but also in Congress and the remainder of the government. The unrestricted sale of public lands continued. The Homestead Acts were blatantly manipulated by private speculators who exploited vast tracts of timber without regard for future needs.

A few voices in and out of the government protested the exploitation of timberlands. Realization had begun to "sink in" that an accelerating rate of timber consumption and waste could not continue forever. In a report by the Commissioner of the General Land Office in 1876, citizens were warned, "A national calamity is being rapidly and surely brought upon the country by the useless destruction of the forests." Referring to the provisions of the Timber Culture Act, it continued,

> . . . it is an anomalous fact that the Government is giving away the rich alluvial soil in Iowa, Nebraska, Kansas, and Minnesota to any citizen who will plant a few acres of cottonwood or other inferior lumber, while under the provisions of the preemption and homestead laws it is

Large West Coast trees required new felling, transportation, and sawing methods. (Courtesy Forest History Society, Santa Cruz, Calif.)

granting a license to destroy millions of acres of pine forests
of almost incalculable value, which should be preserved as
a nation's heritage.[3]

Outside the government, warnings went unheeded. In 1837 a
writer in the *North American Review*, noting the depletion of
southern live oak and New England white pine, stressed the need
to economize remaining wood resources and demanded replace-
ment of the carelessly wasted forests. Local timber shortages
already existed in the East, but only New England shipbuilders
and fur companies had adopted practices that promoted conservation.

Increasing Conservation Concerns

After the Civil War with lumbering more extensive than ever,
the concern for the forests increased, sometimes leading to
overstatements of the situation. For instance, a series of letters in
the *Chicago Tribune* prematurely warned of the exhaustion of
marketable timber in the Great Lakes pine regions. In 1869 a
writer in the *Scientific American* predicted that these pine forests
would all be cut down, and the land would remain desolate. At the
same time published theories purported that the fall of ancient
empires, radical changes of climate, and the spread of epidemics
could be attributed to deforestation. These theories gained
considerable currency, in spite of insufficient evidence. However,
they alerted the public to the importance of the forests and their
relationship to soil erosion, streamflow, and minor variations in
weather conditions. The erosion of cleared land and the narrowing
of stream beds by sedimentation had become common problems.
The theories also recognized the European arguments that a
nation's prosperity and civilization were intimately connected
with its forests. These arguments lay behind European laws that
provided for conservation, fire control, and reforestation. Once the
theories gained acceptance in this country, they led to a
movement for similar laws.

At first the conservation movement confined itself to
scientists, academicians, and journalists, whose influence in
Congress did not compare to that of the opposition. The
acquisition of forest lands by the government, intended to preserve
shipbuilding timbers, had been authorized by Congress early in

the 19th century. It failed, however, to provide funds and subsequent legislation to prevent the routine pillaging of the government land by private interests. The best the Interior Department could do after its creation in 1850 was to send agents to collect payment from the lumber companies for the government timber they had logged. At the same time, other forested public land meant for homesteaders fell into the hands of private speculators.

The conservation movement gained momentum, and by the 1870s influenced state legislatures and then the Federal Government. In the East where forests were thought to be in danger of depletion from the exploitation and destruction by fires, legislatures not only set up special commissions to study the forests but also created state forestry departments. On the western plains a tree-planting movement developed, and societies were founded to promote it. In 1872 Nebraska proclaimed Arbor Day, now a national event. Throughout the plains trees were planted for ornamental and protective purposes. Railroads and commercial enterprises started tree plantations. The interest in tree planting on the plains was reflected in the Timber Culture Act passed by Congress in 1873. This Act conferred title to 160 acres of public land if 40 acres were planted with trees. This Act, however, was also difficult to carry out.

While tree planting was becoming popular, the important concept of scientific forest management developed. In 1873 Franklin B. Hough of New York delivered an address on American forests and national welfare to the American Association for the Advancement of Science. He proposed the Government teach forestry to students and farmers, revise taxes to discourage careless lumbering, and establish forest reserves. A special committee with Hough as chairman was created to promote the cultivation of timber and preserve the forests by informing legislatures of forestry methods. The information the special committee sent to Congress and the President was a first step that led to the eventual creation of the U.S. Forest Service. Congress appropriated $2,000 for a study of forest and lumber production, and commissioned Hough to write the first of his influential *Reports on Forestry* that appeared in 1876.

In 1877 Carl Schurz was appointed Secretary of the Interior by President Hayes and began to take stronger measures against what he called the wicked and wanton waste of timber on public lands. Schurz set up a forestry agency in the Department of the Interior; this agency eventually became the Division of Forestry in the Department of Agriculture. He sent representatives to Europe to study forestry practices.

A national forestry association, later to be called the American Forestry Association, was organized in Philadelphia in 1875. In 1882 the American Forest Congress met for the first time in Cincinnati, Ohio, with B. E. Fernow the first secretary. Fernow became the Chief of the Forestry Division. The policies Fernow instituted were based on the stated aims of the Forestry Congress for a business-like and conservative use and treatment of forest resources. These policies included federal and state legislation and administration of forests, promotion of knowledge of conservation and reforestation, and proper utilization of forest products. Within a few years forestry courses were inaugurated at a number of American colleges.

The Federal forestry agency in its early stages served only as an information service. It had no power to interfere with timber theft on government land, which Congress was not much interested in stopping. Although Congress had in 1872 made the first direct appropriation for the protection of public timberlands, in 1876 it turned down an attempt to create specifically defined national forests along major rivers. Not until the early 20th century in President Theodore Roosevelt's administration was the present system of national forests established. The closest precedent was Yellowstone National Park, created in 1876; the principle, however, was the federal preservation of a "scenic" rather than a "commercial" forest. In 1885 a mixture of recreational and commercial interests led to the first major state forest, the Adirondack Forest Preserve in New York. Finally, in 1891, Congress empowered the President to declare government-owned forest lands public reservations; this led directly to the national forests.

New Lumber Industry

The early conservation movement responded to the dangers or potential dangers created by rapid and careless lumbering. But the positive contributions of the lumber industry at this time

"Forestry is the preservation of forests by wise use," said President Theodore Roosevelt in 1902. With him is Gifford Pinchot, chief of the Bureau of Forestry. (Wood cut on end grain maple by John Killebrew, Forest Prod. Lab., 1950)

Ox teams remove log from West Coast forest on a skidroad in 1892. (Courtesy Weyerhaeuser Company, Tacoma, Wash.)

cannot be overlooked. Without the rapid expansion of lumbering, the prairies and the far west could not have been settled so rapidly. To meet the rising demand for inexpensive wood, the lumber industry had to move quickly and to be bold and resourceful. Under the circumstances lumbering was bound to be a financially risky, ruthless business as were other frontier enterprises. As lumbering moved westward, the industry, although still largely composed of small operations, had collectively become a great industry that ranked with the railroad and the iron industries. Fortunes in lumbering were made and lost. The general tendency was toward consolidation — larger holdings and larger sawmills.

Early in the 19th century, New York surpassed Maine in lumbering; later Pennsylvania became the leading state. By 1876 Michigan was by far the most productive state, with more than 1,500 timber camps and sawmills employing more than 20,000. Pennsylvania was second in production, followed by Wisconsin and New York. Michigan lumber was sent down the Erie Canal to the eastern seaports and Europe. As the plains were settled, sawmill towns and lumber depots sprang up along the Mississippi River. LaCrosse, Prairie du Chien, Dubuque, Rock Island, St. Louis, and Hannibal all prospered from the lumber trade.

The midwestern focal point for the trade was Chicago, which received lumber over the lakes from the north woods, and from there shipped it by rail. Chicago itself required immense quantities of wood for rebuilding after the 1871 fire. In 1872 it was said that Chicago handled enough lumber to cover 3,000 acres 20 feet deep.[4]

The Lake States remained the center of the lumber industry until the early 20th century, when their magnificent stands of virgin white pine were finally exhausted. The major lumbering operations then shifted to the southern pine belt, but in 1876 these vast pine forests were just beginning to be opened by the railroads. Soon after the Civil War, about 50 sawmills were established near Augusta, Georgia, and a number of large mills were built in northern Florida. Mobile, Alabama, became a major lumber port. Southern lumber regions exported cypress and live oak as well as pine.

In the West small lumbering operations already cut into the redwood forests of northern California. Cutting of sequoias had

Rough lumber was often produced in portable steam-powered saw mills located near the timber supply. (Courtesy Oshkosh Public Museum, Oshkosh, Wis.)

Rafts of rough sawn lumber float down the Wisconsin River to the waiting markets on the Mississippi. (Courtesy State Historical Society of Wisconsin)

begun as early as the Gold Rush in 1849, and many San Francisco mansions were constructed of their wood. In 1852 the California state legislature had turned down a bill to create redwood reserves. After the Civil War public forest lands were allowed to pass rapidly into private hands. There were sawmills along the California coast from Monterey to Eureka, and some of the lumber was shipped as far as Australia and the Pacific islands. After 1860 lumbering operations extended farther north into the dense forests around Puget Sound. As in earlier days, much timber continued to be taken illegally from government land.

The lumber camps developed a life of their own, which Walt Whitman described in his "Song of the Broad-Axe":

> Lumbermen in their winter camp, day-break in the woods, stripes of snow on the limbs of trees, the occasional snapping,
> The glad clear sound of one's own voice, the merry song, the natural life of the woods, the strong day's work,
> The blazing fire at night, the sweet taste of supper, the talk, the bed of hemlock-boughs and the bear skin . . .[5]

The camps also had, in their tall stories about Paul Bunyan, their own folklore. These stories originated in the Northeast between 1850 and 1870, and grew taller and more numerous as they followed the camps to the Great Lakes region. They eventually spread and continued to flourish in southern and western forests. Lumberjacks generally worked in winter in isolated camps. Timber cruisers explored and mapped the woods, noting species, quality, and logging conditions; lumberjacks used these maps, cut the timber, and dragged it to riverbanks. In spring logs were branded to identify the owner and floated downstream to sawmills.

About 1876 a number of inventions made logging faster and more efficient. The double-bitted "Yankee ax" was introduced after 1860; the spiked cant hook for handling logs was perfected about 1870. In 1876 lumberjacks were just beginning to use saws to fell trees. There were also new measuring devices and improved log wagons and rafts.

By the 1860s sawmills, too, had been made more efficient by technical progress. Turbine wheels and steam engines had superseded water wheels in large midwestern and southern mills, although the smaller eastern mills continued to use waterpower.

In this early-day logging scene, a woods crew and steam donkey are being hauled by flatcar from one logging site to the next. (Courtesy Weyerhaeuser Company, Tacoma, Wash.)

Ingenious systems of water-filled wood flumes were designed to carry the heavy West Coast logs to water transportation points below. (Courtesy Forest History Society, Santa Cruz, Calif.)

Circular saws replaced the old single-bladed upright saws and were in turn being replaced by bandsaws. A long bandsaw and a combined jig-bandsaw for ornamental carving were exhibited at the Centennial Exhibition in Philadelphia. Gangsaws with as many as 54 saws were in use by this time.

Numerous devices were developed for specialized cutting: scroll saws, cylinder saws for stave making, planers, and sandpapering and shingle machines. Quartersawing, the cutting of logs on radial lines from the center, which reduced the tendency of boards to warp, also began in the 1870s. The many technical improvements reduced the price of lumber and helped accelerate the urban development of the United States.

Forest Products in Industry

Most industrial uses of wood in 1776 were continued on a larger scale 100 years later. In the North especially, the tanning industry had begun to use hemlock bark extensively as well as oak bark. In the South sumac leaves were sometimes used for tanning and dyeing. There were about 7,500 tanneries, most of them in Pennsylvania and New York. The manufacture of naval stores continued to flourish in the South, especially in North Carolina. The yellow pines provided the main source. About 10,000 trees produced 50 barrels of turpentine and 200 barrels of rosin. Pyroligneous acid, or wood vinegar, was also a product of some southern pine wood distilleries.

Coal, the concentrated remnant of prehistoric forests, was gradually replacing charcoal as an industrial fuel. The charcoal industry, however, while suffering from wood shortages and gradual decline, remained important. The industry had almost exhausted surrounding woodlands in the East; by 1876 it was concentrated in Michigan and the South, where supplies of wood were still adequate. Iron foundries followed this industry to these regions, since charcoal iron was the best available. After 1869, however, charcoal iron's share of the market was increasingly surpassed by that of coal and coke iron.

Charcoal was still most commonly made in earth-covered pits in the woods amid its source of supply or in special conical or oblong brick kilns. Oak made the best charcoal. An acre of black oak yielded 1,000 bushels of charcoal; about 50 bushels of charcoal

New woodworking machinery found ready markets in the rapidly expanding lumber industry. (Courtesy State Historical Society of Wisconsin)

The rosin yards in Savannah, Georgia, in 1903. The old methods of gathering rosin and turpentine are still in use but increasing amounts of naval stores are being obtained as a byproduct of the kraft production of paper pulp. (Photo by U.S. Forest Service)

Hardwood charcoal for a nearby iron furnace was made in this set of kilns in Green Bay, Wisconsin, in 1875. (Courtesy State Historical Society of Wisconsin)

were required to process one ton of iron ore. Chestnut, hickory, other hardwoods, and pine were also converted to charcoal. Apart from fuel, charcoal had other industrial uses. Since it conducts electricity fairly well, charcoal was used in electrical circuits. Charcoal could also absorb noxious gases and fumes and serve as a filter to purify water and other liquids.

Wood was indispensable for structural purposes in many industries. The increasing number of coal, copper, and gold mines required millions of tunnel timbers, or mine props, and wood rails. After the first oil had been drilled at Titusville, Pennsylvania, in 1859, derricks were constructed of hardwoods and storage tanks of cypress. The expanding telegraph system needed 300,000 poles each year. Frames of many industrial machines were of wood. In chemical industries wood vats held corrosive chemicals. Wood barrels were still used for shipping liquids of all kinds. Many important chemicals were distilled from hardwoods: acetic acid, wood alcohol, acetone, creosote, formaldehyde, phenols, and tars. Wood charred at high temperatures yielded a gas suitable for illuminating purposes.

Wood for Fuel

Growing America needed vast quantities of wood for fuel. Wood burning locomotives and river steamers frequently stopped for fuel supplies. Wood gradually gave way to coal as this fuel became available. Wood burning iron parlor stoves, some of elaborate design with "isinglass" windows, were a source of both pride and heat. After the parlor stove came wood or coal fired central heating systems. The kitchen range, made of cast or malleable iron with an integral oven and warming ovens, provided a measure of temperature control through judicious selection of wood and control of dampers. The attached "reservoir" supplied warm water.

Often a byproduct of land clearing operations, firewood was available in rural areas for the asking and often without this formality. The only requirement for making trees into firewood was a great deal of hard work and time to dry the product. In urban areas fuelwood became an article of commerce. Ulysses S. Grant once eked out a precarious living by selling and delivering fuelwood in St. Louis. The steam powered sawmills and wood

processing plants used waste wood for fuel and sold surplus wood to area homes and industries. Since the supply of waste wood exceeded demand, a waste burner was an integral part of the larger early sawmills.

Paper from Wood

The most important of the new industrial uses of wood was in papermaking. The introduction of woodpulp paper had a revolutionary effect. Until this time paper was made from rags, which were relatively expensive. The rag supply soon fell short of the growing needs of the papermaking industry. Since the end of the 18th century efforts had been made to use wood as a substitute for rags. In 1794 Matthew Lyon of Vermont made paper from a mixture of basswood bark and rags. In 1830 two Pennsylvanians made paper woodpulp by using aspen wood and lime. But these methods and others like them proved too inefficient for adoption on a large commercial scale.

About the middle of the 19th century, experiments led to three commercially feasible processes for making woodpulp. About 1855 Hugh Burgess of England and Morris Kean of Philadelphia developed *the soda process*. The wood was cut into chips, boiled in a caustic soda solution under high-pressure steam, washed, filtered, and bleached with chlorine; this produced a pulp that could be mixed with rags or straw to make paper. In 1864 Burgess and Kean established the American Wood Paper Company at Philadelphia, an event that received local attention. Using poplar from Pennsylvania, the mill turned out paper that was 80 percent wood. Other mills were soon built, and when a shortage of local poplar developed, the wood was imported from Maine. Later, mills began to follow the supply of wood to Maine, New Hampshire, and Michigan.

In Germany also about 1855, Heinrich Voelter perfected *the groundwood process*, which became the chief method of producing woodpulp. Pieces of wood are forced against a grindstone, and a stream of water washes away the ground pulp fibers. Introduced to this country in 1866, groundwood papermills numbered about 25 to 30 by 1876. The preferred wood was again poplar, but spruce, pine, basswood, and birch were also used.

In the 1860s Benjamin Tilghman of Pennsylvania ex-

RECORDER

CHEAPEST DAILY ON EARTH--3 CENTS PER WEEK.

VOL. 9. NO. 74. CLEVELAND, FRIDAY, JULY 21, 1899 PRICE ONE CENT.--On Trains 2 Cents.

DYNAMITE!

Attempt Made to Blow Up the Lake View Car Barns.

REWARD

Of $500 Is Offered By the Board of Control.

POLICE WERE POWERLESS

Mob of Rioters on Willson-Av Was Too Strong for Them.

BRYAN

Made a Speech for Harmony at the Chicago Mass Meeting.

CAR BLOWN UP.

Terrific Explosion Beneath a Loaded Trolley on Prospect-St.

SETTLED.

The Suburban Trainmen and Everett Fixed Things Up.

RIOTERS IN COURT.

Judge Fiedler Discharged a Teamster Charged With Soliciting Passengers.

ON THE SICK LIST.

20 PER CENT OF OUR FORCES UNFIT FOR SERVICE.

SHAFTER AND ALGE

THE INCONSISTENCY OF

The world's cheapest newspaper—made possible by the newly available wood pulp newsprint. (Courtesy State Historical Society of Wisconsin) perimented with *the sulfite process,* a process perfected in Sweden. A solution of sulfurous acid and lime dissolves some of the cellular matter of the wood and leaves the fiber to be turned into pulp. The first sulfite pulpmill was established in 1882 in Providence; by 1890 more than 12 successful mills existed.

At first woodpulp paper met resistance as an unproved novelty, but once accepted, its inexpensiveness had a revolutionary effect on journalism and publishing. Newspapers once limited to 4 pages and sold for 5 or 10 cents a copy early in the 1870s, expanded to 10 pages or more and sold for 1 or 2 cents by the end of the decade. The papers increased their news coverage, advertising, and circulation; thus, the newspapers greatly increased their political and social influence. Book paper fell from 24 cents to 7 cents a pound. The greatly increased availability of printed matter encouraged the spread of literacy at a time when a large proportion of the population could not read.

The development of inexpensive woodpulp paper stimulated a wide range of paper manufacturers. Cardboard and wallpaper were soon being made from wood-based paper, as were new products such as paper collars and bonnets, battery jars, and insulation. Paper and paste were compacted by hydraulic pressure into a hard, solid mass resembling ebony and made into doorframes and window frames, barrels, and even, with steel hubs and rims, into railroad wheels. The paper wheels, more elastic than iron wheels, reduced vibration and made less noise, which made them especially suitable for sleeping cars. By absorbing shocks better, they reduced wear on cars. The Allen Paper Carwheel Company, with large factories in Hudson, New York, and Pullman, Illinois, sold 13,000 of these wheels in a single year.

Wood in Travel

The railroads, of course, used wood for a multitude of purposes. Wood was fuel and kindling. Wood became tracks and ties, cars, bridges, trestles, tunnel linings, sheds, and stations. The first railroad tracks were wood planks or rails, sometimes topped with spiked-down strap iron. In 1876 some of these old wood roads were still being used in remote areas, and wood railroads were still being built to serve mines and lumber camps. Each year railroads required millions of new crossties. Locust ties lasted longest, 15 to 20 years; yellow pine, cypress, and cedar, sometimes used, lasted 8 to 10 years. The most common ties were of white oak and of chestnut, which, until preservatives came into use, had to be replaced every 7 years. To insure a supply of wood for ties and for fuel, railroads began tree plantations. They also planted trees along tracks to provide windbreaks and shade and to encourage settlement.

In the 1860s at its peak as a fuel, wood was burned by railroads in prodigious amounts. In 1869 all American locomotives combined burned 19,000 cords of wood a day. On the Lake Shore and Michigan Southern Railroad, one cord of white oak, beech, or maple was required to cover 48 miles. Wood was used for kindling in coal-burning locomotives and in stoves in passenger cars to provide heat during the winter. Although by 1876 coal was becoming the standard railroad fuel, locomotives still commonly burned wood, especially in the South and in the north woods where supply was plentiful.

Pullman day cars, light wood passenger cars, were introduced in 1858, while Pullman sleepers and dining cars appeared after the Civil War. These cars soon became as luxurious as the interior of a Victorian mansion, replete with mahogany paneling and elaborate decorative carving.

New types of public transportation in cities — horsecars, electric trolleys, and cable cars — were made mostly of wood, as were private carriages and buggies. In the 1870s the old style of private carriage, with small front wheels and low axles, gave way to a more streamlined model. Front wheels, almost as large as rear wheels, allowed the carriage to run more smoothly. American buggies had a good reputation overseas as well as at home for being lightweight, inexpensive vehicles. The two-wheeled velocipede had "caught on" in the 1860s, and a school for training prospective riders opened in New York.

Eastern coachmakers still had the reputation for producing the finest coaches and carriages in the country, but the manufacture of wagons as well as pleasure vehicles was also well established in the Midwest and West. Conestoga wagons, farm and freight wagons, and carts were turned out by large, mechanized factories, with specialized machines to produce every part of a vehicle.

Plank Roads

Roads were better than they had been 100 years earlier but still needed to be improved. The plank road offered temporary success in the 1850s. At first a rival of the railroads, it later became a smoother way of reaching the railroad terminals. Plank roads were turnpikes with tollgates to provide revenue for upkeep. Companies chartered to build these roads depended on state laws for assistance.

The roads consisted of planks 8 feet long and 3 or 4 inches thick laid across two or four parallel rows of timbers embedded in the earth. In the North hemlock, oak, elm, and beech were the woods primarily used, and in the South, pine. In good condition these plank roads were the smoothest in America until the concrete roads of this century, and they were less expensive than any other pavements of that period. Horses or mules could draw two or three times the load on plank roads than they could on broken stone pavement or ordinary roads. Less wear resulted on vehicles. Therefore, plank roads became popular with farmers, and adjacent farmland increased in value. Unfortunately, backers had underestimated their rate of deterioration. Expected to last 10 years with repairs, plank roads averaged about 5. When holes formed, the roads were dangerous or impassable; the companies found it difficult to keep them repaired. Consequently few plank roads were built after 1857.

During the 10 years in which plank roads were popular, they were built throughout the country. Two thousand miles of wood roads were built in New York. Michigan, Wisconsin, and other midwestern states had extensive systems. In some states, such as Alabama, plank roads delayed the coming of railroads, but the extension of railroads and the deterioration of the plank roads eventually brought about their demise. A few wood roads remained in 1876, however. Some of Chicago's streets were still paved with planks, because stone pavement tended to sink into swampy ground. Several of the plank roads to the surrounding prairie also remained in use.

Covered and Uncovered Bridges

When a road reached a stream, a traveler of 1876, unlike a

Logging railroads were the prime movers of men, machinery, and logs in the Pacific Northwest from the 1890s to the 1940s. (Courtesy Forest History Society, Santa Cruz, Calif.)

A steam donkey engine powers a cable yarding system to drag logs to a centralized location. (Courtesy Forest History Society, Santa Cruz, Calif.)

traveler of 1776, would likely find a sound and sophisticated wood bridge, open or covered. Iron bridges were just appearing, although most bridges were still built of wood. The first known American covered bridge had been a 550-foot, three-span bridge built by Timothy Palmer at Philadelphia in 1805. The covered bridge soon thereafter became a familiar feature of the American landscape, an emblem of small-town life. The bridge was not covered to protect the user, to keep his horse from shying at the sight of water, or to keep snow off the floor. The cover protected the wood framework of the bridge itself. If the supporting structural timbers or trusses were kept dry, the bridge would endure as evidenced by the condition of many of the covered bridges today. More than 1,500 covered bridges can still be found in the United States and Canada.

Covered bridges were commonly built by ordinary carpenters who used only handtools and exerted much skill and ingenuity. Almost any kind of wood might be chosen: white oak, pine, fir, hemlock, or cedar. Many railroad bridges were covered. In small towns, the covered bridge served as play areas for children, a place for advertisements, public meetings, and courtship. It was not surprising they acquired the appellation "kissing bridges."

Several important advances in bridge engineering originated during the early 19th century. Laminated structural members were introduced in 1805 in the Trenton Bridge spanning the Delaware River. Ithiel Town, in 1819, developed the Town Bridge with latticework trusses, which allowed lighter than customary timbers to be used. In 1840 William Howe patented a parallel-chord truss that permitted a complete stress analysis by mathematical method. These valuable structural innovations were incorporated in the wood bridges built during the 1870s. Concurrently, engineers developed methods of preserving timber by injecting creosote and other chemicals under pressure. This greatly increased the lifespan not only of bridges, but also of piers, docks, retaining walls, and other wood structures exposed to water.

End of Shipbuilding Era

Advances had been made in shipbuilding in the 100 years since the United States declared its independence. The paddlewheel steamboat dominated the traffic on the Ohio, Mississippi, and other major rivers. This type of boat was built of oak, walnut, yellow-poplar, and other woods; it consumed wood for fuel in immense quantities. The boilers in the largest steamboats required a cord of hardwood each hour. These boats stopped frequently at river ports to replenish their supply of maple, oak, hickory, pecan, and other firewood. Barges and rafts were still on the rivers; canal boats traveled numerous canals dug early in the century. Sailing yachts for recreation were appearing on coastal waters and lakes.

The advent of steam-powered oceangoing ships that used coal as fuel spelled an end to the era of wood sailing ships, but especially in the United States, the end came slowly. Although by the 1880s iron steamships had begun to dominate foreign fleets, the U.S. Navy wood sailing ships prevailed until the turn of the century in American shipyards and merchant fleets. Until then wood sailing ships were still necessary for long trading voyages, such as those around South America and Africa where there were no adequate coal stations for steamships.

American shipyards, which could not profitably compete with European shipyards in iron construction, continued to produce relatively cheap wood ships. Consequently, as the number of sailing ships declined and were gradually replaced by steamships on even the longer trade routes, the number of American shipyards declined. The shipyards also produced wood steamships, but since wood hulls did not always hold up well against the vibrations of the larger engines, iron construction was increasingly favored for oceangoing steamers. Wood paddlewheel steamers continued to be purchased, however, for trade on the coasts and on the Great Lakes. Even for iron ships, wood was still needed. Iron fouled badly with long exposure to seawater; iron hulls were often sheathed with layers of wood or wood was sandwiched between an iron hull and an outer copper sheathing.

In the last age of wood sailing ships, the fast and romantic clipper ships appeared. Toward the end of the 19th century, the largest sailing ships in history, the merchant ships, were built in Maine. The American clipper flourished in the 1850s on the Atlantic crossing and particularly on the long trip to California around the Cape. It was designed for speed, with a long, sleek hull and a great expanse of sail. It could average 18

"Summer Scenes in New York Harbor" is the title of this 1883 lithograph by Currier & Ives. (Courtesy of Mystic Seaport, Inc., Mystic, Conn. Photo by Mary Anne Stets.)

miles per hour, covering more than 400 miles in 24 hours; in full sail it was a graceful and an exhilarating sight.

In the 1870s the competition of steamships and the general economic conditions culminated in the virtual extinction of wood shipbuilding south of Cape Cod. Norfolk, Baltimore, Philadelphia, New York, and the cities of southern New England almost ceased building oceangoing vessels. Many shipbuilders went bankrupt, yards closed, and shipwrights moved on or did only repair work. Even in Massachusetts, the output of deep-sea ships in the 1870s was less than half of that of the 1850s.

Only in Maine, with its stable rural economy, its local supply of timber, and especially its relatively cheap labor costs, did shipbuilding remain prosperous. By 1875 Maine shipyards produced 80 percent of the square-rigged ships built in the United States, although even in Maine production had declined 50 percent since the 1850s. But the standard ships being built there, great wood cargo ships for carrying grain, were three times as large as the typical freighters of the clipper ship era. In the 1870s, vessels of more than 2,000 tons were common; in the 1880s, a number of 3,000-ton ships were built in the Bath, Thomaston, Rockport, and Kennebunkport yards. In 1892 one of the larger American wood sailing ships ever built, the 3,539-ton *Roanoke,* was completed at Bath. The builders believed that it had the greatest size and efficiency attainable in a wood ship.

The vessels built in the remaining eastern shipyards during the 1870s were of timbers assembled from throughout the United States. The necessity of transporting wood from distant virgin forests was a factor that not only made shipbuilding less profitable, but untenable. Except in Maine and a few isolated spots, the supply of ship timbers in the forests along the coast had been virtually exhausted.

In the construction of large ships for hauling grain, from 200 to 300 great white oaks were required; these trees had become rare in the Northeast. The heavy frame pieces, therefore, increasingly had to be brought from the remaining white oak stands in coastal and interior regions of Maryland and Virginia and from the oak woods of the Ohio Valley, the Great Lakes States, and Ontario. Live oak was still occasionally used as a floor timber, and was obtained in Florida. Knees were made of hackmatack (tamarack) or spruce, softwoods from northern Maine or New Brunswick,

Canada. Hardwoods, primarily maple, beech, and birch, were used in top timbers and other parts of the ship. The planking was usually hard southern pine or white oak.

With the depletion of the great white pines in the East, mast timbers had to be obtained from the stands of virgin white pine in the Lake States or from the pine forests of the southern states and the state of Oregon. Shipbuilders usually were compelled to hire timber contractors who went into the woods with the ship specifications and supervised cutting. This, unfortunately, added time and expense to the increasing costs and difficulties that beset shipbuilders in the 1870s. Only in Maine did most shipyards survive the difficulties.

Household Objects of Wood

Iron was invading small manufactures, tools, and domestic ware as well as shipbuilding; yet in 1876 as in 1776 most of the implements, instruments, and utensils were still wholly or partly of wood. This was especially true in the country, where whittling woodenware continued to be a customary pastime.

In the country trees remained a source of folk remedies and dyes, the lore passed on from generation to generation. Maple sugar reached peak production in 1880 and was produced not only in the Northeast but as far south and west as Tennessee and Missouri. Trees were cultivated more than ever before for shade, windbreaks, and ornament. At Christmas the custom of bringing an evergreen tree into the home and decorating it, introduced by German immigrants in the 1840s, had become an American tradition.

On the plains where no local wood was available for fencing, the small, thorny, osage-orange tree served as an efficient hedge. Barbed wire, invented in 1873, eventually replaced hedges, but even then wood was needed for posts.

In a home among much traditional woodenware, a number of items had appeared since 1776 and were at least partly made of wood: sewing machines with walnut tables, ironing boards, washing machines, iceboxes, ice cream freezers, and coffee grinders. Metal tools and implements of all kinds, from icepicks to umbrellas, had wood handles, as did brushes, dusters, and brooms. Clocks, whether a large grandfather clock or a mantel clock, still had wood casing.

Many small wood manufactures were new: matchsticks, pencils, rulers, pipes, and baseball bats. Factories specializing in small wood items were concentrated in New England. A single establishment in Burlington, Vermont, produced 4,000 bushels of shoe pegs a day. A small factory district in Maine produced two-thirds of the spools used in the United States.

Winchendon, Massachusetts, claimed it manufactured more woodenware than any other town in the world; the value of its products was more than $1 million annually. Remote New England hill villages turned out all varieties of woodenware. Many of these small establishments found toys a profitable sideline and produced children's wheelbarrows, carts, sleds, and rocking horses.

Musical instruments had become an important manufacture from wood. American pianos, which won two gold medals and attracted much attention at the Paris Exhibition of 1867, were unexcelled by those of any other country. New York probably led the world in piano manufacturing. As early as 1865 some 70 establishments were producing between 250 and 300 instruments a week. In 1870 more than 24,000 pianos were manufactured in the United States; this volume probably exceeded that of any other country. In the same year an even larger number of small household organs were produced; of the 29,000 reported in the census, about half were produced in Massachusetts and 3,000 in Vermont. At about the same time, a 60-foot-high organ was made of black walnut for the Boston Music Hall; the wood was embellished with mythological figures and busts of composers.

Furnituremaking: Craft and Industry

In 1876 in remote small towns carpenters and joiners still made the furniture. Sometimes 18th century styles were still followed in the simple pine cupboards and chests; hickory and oak chairs and rockers; and maple four-poster beds, kitchen tables, and six-leg tables with tapered maple legs. No ornamentation was used except perhaps stenciled designs on surfaces. Pine, maple, and cherry were still the species most frequently chosen.

In general, early in the 19th century large furniture workshops, which resembled factories where labor was distributed among skilled and unskilled workers, had begun to replace the individual craftsman's shop. After 1850 furniture factories with steam-driven machinery multiplied, particularly in areas close to the lumber industry. By 1836 furniture was being manufactured in Grand Rapids, Michigan, which soon became a center of the industry. As demand increased, mass-produced, machine-made furniture completely dominated the market. By 1877 a writer in *The American Cabinet Maker*, a trade journal, stated with only slight exaggeration, "The days are gone, never to return, when an individual art workman could be employed on an individual piece of furniture to do what he liked with it."

Furniture ceased to have the aesthetic distinction of the 18th century. Machinery could not equal the mastery and imagination of the individual craftsman. Furthermore, the advantage of a pure, universal style was lost. Virtually all styles that had ever been fashionable were revived during the Victorian period and mixed and superimposed to the point of chaos. A typical Victorian room, cluttered and overdecorated, showed a taste for lavish, ostentatious embellishment. Large furniture companies competed with each other to pile ornament upon ornament, which resulted in conglomerations of Greek, Turkish, Gothic, Renaissance, Empire, and Egyptian motifs.

Elaborately curved, intricately carved designs first became popular in the 1840s in the furniture of John Belter of New York City. Belter was a skillful carver. Because an ordinary board could not sustain the delicate, lacy carved patterns Belter preferred, he used plywood. He glued together from 3 to 16 thin layers of rosewood, oak, black walnut, or ebonized hardwood, each about 1/16-inch thick, so that the grain of a given layer ran at a right angle to the adjacent layers. He then frequently steamed the panels in molds to achieve the sinuous curves characteristic of his work.

The use of veneer in furniture was fairly new, although it had been used for furniture by the ancient Egyptians. In America an early important use of veneer was in laminated grand piano rims, first introduced about 1830 and generally accepted by 1860. Plywood, made by orienting adjacent plies at right angles to each other, came into use for plywood chair and seatbacks in 1875, and for tops and fronts of furniture in 1885 to 1900. In 1840 the first veneer-cutting lathe was patented in America by John Dresser; by 1875 a veneer slicer had been developed.

By the middle of the 19th century, dozens of new woodworking machines were introduced, including steam-driven planers, mortisers, and wood-carving and fret-cutting machines. At this time the circular saw came into general use. It could cut large sheets of thin lumber or veneer, which were used to cover soft secondary woods in large pieces of cabinet furniture. The bandsaw was widely adopted after 1870. The advent of power-driven saws and carving machines completed the trend toward mechanization and mass production in the furniture industry. This made fashionable furniture available to the middle-income families as well as to the high income. The new machines also completed the trend toward extravagant ornamentation and the revival of past styles.

After the massive, ornate Renaissance style was popularized by Grand Rapids furniture companies, other historical and new exotic styles became fashionable in rapid succession. Within these styles, there were notable artistic achievements, as in some Renaissance chairs and cabinets made in New York. In general, however, the styles were overwrought or combined in ponderous confusion, and furniture design declined. In the 1870s the latest fashion was the Gothic Eastlake style. Originally intended as a reform, it soon became encrusted with fussy ornamentation. The preferred woods were mahogany, rosewood, and walnut.

In reaction to the stylistic deformities in machine-made furniture, a crafts movement emerged in England and then in the United States. Groups of artists and craftsmen, such as the Roycrafters at East Aurora, New York, and the Art Workers Guild of Providence, Rhode Island, produced the most attractive furniture of the time. Architects such as H. H. Richardson began to design furniture harmonious with the houses they designed. Although too expensive and limited in quantity for general consumption, custom made furniture eventually influenced the market.

Toward the end of the 19th century the vogue for oak furniture of plain, massive, rectilinear Mission style was an outgrowth of the crafts movement. Furthermore, amid the elaborate and heavy sideboards, bureaus, dropleaf tables, upholstered chairs, and lampstands that are thought of as typical Victorian furniture, there were some outstanding innovations. Among those that made use of wood were reclining chairs, chairs with metal backs and

The characteristic New England village was reproduced throughout the country. Pictured is Black River Falls, Wisconsin, in the 1890s with churches, homes, buildings, fences, sidewalks, and utility poles, all of wood. (Courtesy State Historical Society of Wisconsin)

legs and wood seats, and canvas folding chairs with x-shaped wood legs.

Toward the end of the 19th century, an interest in 18th century furniture emerged, which in 1876 turned into a "centennial mania" for colonial heirlooms. At the Philadelphia Centennial Exhibition, New England exhibits displayed in wood Georgian-style houses included 100-year-old spinning wheels, mahogany furniture, and grandfather clocks with wood works. The cult of antiques then began in earnest.

People who had not inherited colonial furniture went on antiquing expeditions throughout the countryside. Generally they found Windsor chairs and Queen Anne tables had been consigned to an attic or a henhouse. The country people were undoubtedly astonished when city dwellers offered to buy their most dilapidated furniture. Despite the taste for 18th century antiques, however, Queen Anne and Chippendale were among the few styles not extensively revived in Victorian furniture, probably because they did not lend themselves to rich adornment. At the end of the century, however, the devotion to antiques finally did foster reproductions of colonial styles in machine-made furniture.

Old and New Architecture

The styles of architecture in 1876 bear a resemblance to those of the furniture: very plain on the frontier and in the countryside and villages, extravagantly ornate in the cities and fashionable suburbs and resorts. On the western frontier wherever timber was available and in the southern Appalachians and the Ozarks, the log cabin was still the standard dwelling. Western cattle and mining towns were typified by wood commercial buildings, clapboard houses and churches, wood sidewalks, hitching posts, and corrals. On farms, in small towns, and in many city neighborhoods, plain wood houses were the most common type of dwelling. The characteristic New England village, with shady streets lined with white-painted clapboard houses, was reproduced throughout the country.

Wood remained the principal domestic construction material. An important reason for its continuing success in meeting the housing needs of Americans was the use of the "balloon frame" invented in the 1830s. Prior to this, buildings had been supported

An abundance of wood made America a nation of home owners. Woodcut of Belleville, New Jersey. (Enlarged from Early Woodcut Views of New York and New Jersey, *John W. Barber and Henry Howe, Dover Publications, Inc.)*

A tribute to the ingenuity of the pioneers, the Salt Lake Tabernacle was under construction about 1865. Fastenings were wood pegs reinforced with rawhide. (Courtesy Church of Jesus Christ of Later Day Saints, Salt Lake City, Utah)

by heavy walls or frameworks of heavy timbers; either type required time and skill to construct. Augustine Taylor of Chicago then discovered that a sound structure could be achieved with multiple thin pieces of lumber precisely spaced, braced, and fastened together with a generous number of nails. In fact, the introduction of cheap, machine-produced nails made this building innovation possible.

The first application by Taylor on the new frame theory was a wood church, which was generally expected to collapse but disappointed skeptics by standing. A structure of this kind is, in fact, strong. The cubical framework enabled 2 by 4s to perform like heavy oak timbers used in older buildings. The multiple-member construction and nonweight-bearing walls anticipated the steel-framed skyscraper, the prototypes of which were built, also in Chicago, soon after 1876. The more flexible interior arrangement of Victorian houses was partly due to the introduction of balloon-frame construction. Because this method of construction was less expensive and because of an abundance of inexpensive lumber, this method helped America become a nation of homeowners.

Most of the fashionable styles of architecture in 1876, as in 1776, originated in Europe. Again the chief difference in the American versions was the frequent use of wood in construction. In Victorian architecture as in furniture, elaborate ornamentation was preferred and made possible by wood construction. This gilded age, as it is called, is characterized by the opulent wood Gothic mansions and resort hotels built during the period. A most extravagant and extraordinary example is the mansion built in 1885 by lumber magnate William McKendrie Carson in Eureka, California. Crowded with bizarre multicolored carved ornament outside and inside, it reportedly contains every kind of wood then available in the world market.

About 1876 the Gothic style reached its greatest popularity in the United States. Its characteristic features are tall, often topheavy towers and pinnacles; spires; narrow, pointed windows; a profusion of dormers; steep, sharply peaked gables; and the carved, external woodwork. The general effect is one of complex angularity, strong vertical lines, and pointed, narrow forms — a romantic medieval effect.

Another romantic style called Queen Anne featured steep

This pioneer family has evidently prospered and will soon move from the log cabin home to their fine new wood frame house. Central Wisconsin, 1880. (Courtesy State Historical Society of Wisconsin)

The elaborately ornamented wood mansion of William McKendrie Carson was built in 1885 in California (Photo by H. O. Fleischer)

roofs, towers, and turrets, and "caught on" after a British exhibit at the Philadelphia Centennial Exposition. The style came not from the 18th century when Queen Anne ruled, but from the late Medieval and Tudor periods. Queen Anne houses often had brick lower sections, with the upper sections in the Tudor half-timber style or else entirely of wood with shingles or clapboard sheathing. The style, therefore, offered a variety of colors and textures. The carved wood embellishment, frequently massive and elaborate, might consist of broad friezes with carved leaf decoration and ornate supports under the eaves.

The French Second Empire style was often constructed of wood, as in the California governor's former mansion in Sacramento. Distinctive features include a high mansard roof with arched dormer windows, balconies, windows with ornamental framing, and in general, tall, bold forms, often including a tower.

The adaptation of the Italianate villa style into wood after its introduction about the middle of the 19th century brought about some variations in the design. The great adaptability of wood allowed an architect to suit the particular needs of a client, especially in the interior. The exterior featured wide eaves, window-frame moldings, a prominent gable over the front door, a pillar loggia or gallery, and a square tower.

The Swiss Chalet, one of the imported styles, did not have to be imitated in wood. Swiss prototypes were built entirely of wood. About midcentury, this style appealed to those who favored the picturesque. Gables were wide, eaves broad; there were multiple balconies, exterior stairs, and quaint carved decorations throughout.

Because all of the major European styles were reproduced in wood in this country, it is not surprising that the only two prominent domestic styles of the time that originated in America were styles of wood construction. The "Stick" style, although it reflected the influence of the Gothic style and that of the Swiss Chalet, was an original native style introduced in 1850. In a stick style house the large framing timbers were exposed on the upper stories in rectangular and diagonal patterns, as in the Tudor half-timber house, and the space between covered with clapboards. The projection of the beams was intended to reveal the wood structure and so evince "truthfulness" in architecture, a preoccupation of

A wood carver works on a crude beginning to a fine piece of furniture.
(Courtesy State Historical Society of Wisconsin)

modern architecture. Other features of the style included a high steep roof with projecting eaves and an extensive porch with carved posts. The plan of the house was complex and irregular.

The "Shingle" style originated in the 1870s in New England and derived much of its character from the earliest colonial houses in that area. This style with horizontal forms and quiet, plain exterior contrasted markedly with the prevailing Victorian styles. Generally there was no carved ornamentation. Shingles covered the walls, the gambrel roof, and sometimes even the porch supports. A most distinguished example is the Sherman residence in Newport, Rhode Island. The roof with dormers is steeply pitched and shingled, and the upper story is shingled with cross-timbered sections above the first story of stone. Completed in 1876, the Sherman residence is considered the finest domestic design by H. H. Richardson, one of the most influential American architects.

Woodcarving

The interiors of mansions and hotels of 1876, whether of masonry or wood construction, were decorated with rich paneling and intricate, floral carvings. The carving in many Victorian buildings was by skilled craftsmen who often created designs of high artistic quality.

Shipcarvers were still busy not only in the eastern seaports but on the Great Lakes and the Pacific coast, although the need for their art lessened with the declining fortunes of wood sailing ships. Shipcarving had flourished in the decades dominated by the clippers. Exquisite figureheads by master shipcarvers adorned the sailing ships still being built. For instance the figurehead for the *Belle of Bath* by C.A.L. Sampson of Bath, Maine, is an elegant portrait of the captain's daughter with flowing drapery and scrollwork to express the motion of the waves of the sea. Steamships had no projecting prow for a figurehead to embellish and complete. Although a few early steamships positioned sedate, upright figures at their bows, carving on steamships was generally limited to pilothouse eagles, paddlebox decorations, and rich cabin decorations.

With the decline in commissions for figureheads, some shipcarvers turned to carving cigarstore Indians and similar advertising figures. This carving reached its greatest popularity in the 1870s and 1880s. Not only Indians, but Turks, sailors, baseball players, Uncle Sams, fashionable men and women, policemen, preachers, and famous individuals such as Lord Byron and John L. Sullivan were carved to be placed in front of tobacco stores, all holding cigars or a leaf of tobacco. The carver usually worked with white pine, bought in logs at spar yards; he blocked the figure out with an ax and used a chisel for detail. Hands and arms were attached, and the finished figure painted and set on a wheeled stand. Some of the wood Indians are remarkably realistic.

Professional carvers continued to turn out a variety of appropriate symbols and signs for shops, plaques and portraits for public buildings, religious figures, weathervanes, and sculptural decoration for saloons and for gardens and homes. Samuel Robb, who became the most prolific carver of wood Indians, opened shop in New York in 1876. He produced all varieties of wood carving, including circus carvings for the new Ringling and Barnum traveling circuses. Circus wagons, designed to lure spectators, were lavishly decorated with brightly painted, gilded carved fairytale and mythological figures and circus animals. Carrousels displayed herds of fanciful wood horses and other animals. All of these circus sculptures were of pine wood and given all of the imaginative vitality that artists could summon.

Amateur carvers using jackknives produced notable specimens of American folk art. Wilhelm Schimmel, a German immigrant, was a well-known itinerant carver who wandered the Cumberland Valley in Pennsylvania during the late 19th century. The thousands of small, vigorously carved animals he traded for shelter, board, and rum are now eagerly sought and proudly displayed by collectors and museums. Statues and busts of Lincoln and other patriotic figures are typical creations of the amateur carvers as are religious sculptures, garden statues, flagpole ornaments, and mantlepieces.

Some of the most beautiful carvings still were the bird decoys, an art adopted from the Indians. The bodies of the decoys were of cedar or pine, the heads of a harder wood; and finished carving was finely polished and realistically painted. All kinds of shorebirds — plovers, sandpipers, herons — were imitated as well as ducks. Indian tribes throughout the country continued their traditional wood carving — totem poles, animal and human figures, and decorated woodenware.

With the decline in commissions for figureheads, some wood carvers turned to new challenges. This Lion and Mirror bandwagon, with elaborately carved wood figures, was built about 1879 by the Sebastion Iron Works of New York City. It was used by the Adam Forepaugh Circus (1879-1889), Ringling Brothers Circus (1890-1915), and Cole Brother Circus (1935-1937). (Courtesy Circus World Museum, Baraboo, Wis.)

Sailors on South Sea voyages picked up pieces of mahogany and other exotic woods and carved boxes, canes, pipes, watch holders, and model ships. Whittling continued to be a productive and creative activity on the farm.

Woodblock Engraving

Woodblock illustration dates back to the 15th century. In this type of illustration, a wood block is cut away, leaving a design in relief. In 1876 woodblock engraving was an indispensable art in publishing. It had become the essential medium for every kind of printed illustration, from encyclopedias to illustrated newspapers. Before the invention of photographic printing, only the wood engraver could provide illustrations with the detail and the accuracy needed for catalogs of mass-produced goods, advertisements, magazines, and books, including textbooks. Engravers masterfully copied the drawings of major artists, and made them available to a wide public. In 1876 colored engravings, printed by superimposing images from several individually cut blocks, were just being introduced; they rivaled lithography in accuracy and brilliance. By the 18th century metal plates were used for most illustrations, and woodcuts which were made from softwoods had declined into a cheap and crudely executed method of illustration produced in small workshops for local printers.

Early in the 19th century Thomas Bewick of England discovered that a block of boxwood, a very hard wood with close, even grain, would yield a very finely detailed engraving. This method was at least as accurate as intaglio printing from metal plates and was cheaper and faster; it soon prevailed in the publishing business. Bewick also introduced the technique of working out the picture directly on the block instead of copying drawings. Wood engraving again became a fine art.

In America there were 400 professional engravers by 1870. Illustrated magazines enlisted major artists, such as Winslow Homer, Thomas LaFarge, and Thomas Nast, as well as established engravers, who produced masterpieces of the art. Toward the end of the century, mechanical and photographic methods of reproduction began to replace wood engraving, although they could not equal the capacity of the wood engraving to reproduce minute details. A few engraving establishments survived. The technique was taken up again by artists who worked directly on a woodblock and produced prints of highest artistic quality.

Age of Transition

The year 1876 belonged to an age of transition. It is not surprising that the importance of wood in American life should also have been in a state of transition. Some of the older uses of wood — fuel, pavement, sailing ships, charcoal iron — were diminishing or disappearing. However, the many new uses of wood — for paper, plywood, telegraph and telephone poles, railroads, chemicals — more than made up the loss. Many of the uses in 1776 — construction, furniture, tanning, vehicles, bridges, fencing, musical instruments, art — persisted in 1876, and had grown with the country. The new industrial age — the age of iron, steel, and coal — was still an age of wood.

The adaptability of wood to changing conditions preserved the rich tradition of wood in American life and continued the close and essential relationship of the American people to their forests. The conservation movement that emerged reflected not only an awareness of this relationship, but an awareness that the close relationship could and must endure.

In executing the wood engraving of this tree, Thomas Bewick cut on the end rather than the plank side of the wood, which provided both durability and meticulous detail not available with a woodcut. (Enlarged from 1800 Woodcuts by Thomas Bewick and his School, Blanche Cirker, ed., Dover Publications, Inc.)

PART 3

WOOD
IN THE
INDUSTRIAL
ERA

The solar-heated wood home emerges in response to increasing concerns for energy conservation and wiser use of our natural resources. Home in Madison, Wisconsin. (Photo by JoAnne B. Easton)

1976

A nation of 13 sparsely settled states founded in 1776 has become a nation of 50 states with a population of more than 200 million. Three-fourths of the population is urban or suburban. Each of the three largest cities, New York, Chicago, and Los Angeles, has a larger population than that of the entire country at the time of the Declaration of Independence. The present complex and predominantly urban society of the United States has been made possible by unprecedented exploitation of natural resources and by continuous technological development. During the last 100 years, innovations in transportation, agriculture, communications, and medical care have profoundly affected American life. Civilization now rests on a complex, interdependent industrial economy that requires vast and increasing amounts of energy and raw materials.

In this world of apparent plenty, timber remains one of the raw materials basic to the U.S. economy. During the last four to five decades, annual consumption of wood products has increased 50 percent to a prodigious level of 13.7 billion cubic feet. Forest products industries employ almost 1.8 million and have an annual payroll of 14 billion dollars. Forest industries still retain a strong grass roots complexion. They are highly competitive and involve many enterprises throughout the nation. The 1972 *Census of Manufacturers* reported 33,695 establishments dealing in lumber products.

Accelerating demand for sawed wood products in the 19th century encouraged rapid development of a large sawmilling industry. Production of lumber in 1876 totaled 18 billion board feet, sawed with the aid of the newly invented steam engine. As the nation grew and demanded more and more wood products to build the railroads that crossed the continent and to house the population of the Plains States, so the sawmilling industry grew. At first the industry was based on the seemingly limitless timber supplies of the northern Lake States. By 1906 lumber production had reached a peak of 40 billion board feet. The industry was forced to look elsewhere for timber — to the South, then to the West Coast with its virgin stands of very large timber.

In the rapidly growing lumber industry adventuresome and enterprising people were able to rise rapidly to positions of leadership from humble jobs in woods or mill. One such person was Frederick Weyerhaeuser who arrived in the United States as a penniless immigrant from Germany at the age of 18. He began work at a small sawmill in Rock Island, Illinois. The company promptly failed, and in 1858 the young immigrant was put in charge of a salvage effort. With his brother-in-law, F. C. A. Denkmann, he soon became owner of the plant and turned it into a profitable venture. Later the partners organized the Mississippi River Logging Company to get better control of timber supplies. Soon they had extensive timberland holdings in the Lake States.

In 1899 Weyerhaeuser visited the Pacific Northwest to have a look at the 245 billion board feet of timber then standing west of the Cascade Mountains. It was here in 1825 that a young Scotch botanist by the name of David Douglas, following reports of the fabulous timber resources brought back by Lewis and Clark in 1805, had collected specimens of an unknown conifer that was to become known as Douglas-fir. The tree is not a true fir. Scientists called it by a Latin name that meant "false hemlock with the leaf of a yew." The fact that it never received a proper name unique to its species did not prevent it from becoming the most important timber tree of the 20th century.

Within a few months the foresighted Weyerhaeuser had arranged to purchase 900,000 acres of land from the Northern Pacific Railroad at $6 an acre, and the fabulous story of the expansion of one of America's largest private timber enterprises had begun. This firm and other American forest products

The first West Coast Weyerhaeuser Mill in Everett, Washington, about 1902. (Courtesy, Weyerhaeuser Company, Tacoma, Wash.)

industries now own and harvest timber on about 14 percent, or 67 million acres, of the nation's most productive forest land.

Another interesting partnership was that of Robert A. Long and Victor Bell. These young men found themselves engaged in an unprofitable business of selling hay in Kansas in 1874. They solved their economic problems by tearing down their hay storage sheds and selling the lumber. The surprisingly good profits from the sale convinced them that the lumber business was worthy of their talents. The Long-Bell Company soon owned over 50 lumber outlets in the Midwest that were sufficiently profitable to enable it to buy timberland in the South and West and to build and operate lumber and plywood manufacturing plants.

With the depression in 1932 annual sawmill output dropped to a low level of 13.5 billion board feet. During World War II production recovered to an annual level of about 40 billion board feet where it remains. An estimated 50,000 sawmills were operating after World War II, but many of these were small and inefficient. At present about 12,000 sawmills, many of them new, large, and efficient, are operating.

The source of most of today's supply of wood is the 500 million acres classified as commercial forest land; this is about 22 percent of the total U.S. land area. The increased yield of products from the shrinking forest land base reflects the results of reforestation, improved management, growth, control of fires, and better manufacturing methods.

Wood has retained many traditional uses. Although new uses have developed to meet new needs and new and improved wood products have entered the market, the changes brought about by improved technology have been ushered in gradually. Only by careful retrospection can there be understanding of the scope and the significance of the dramatic changes in managing, harvesting, manufacturing, and using the U.S. forest resource. Two significant and parallel developments are of special importance in understanding how change has come about. One is the industrialization of the forest products industries; the other, the growth of research on which industrialization depends.

Industrialization of Forest Products Manufacture

Compared to developments in the minerals and metals industries during the past century, it may appear that industrialization in the wood industries progressed slowly. Perhaps, because wood always had been so widely used, so well known, so readily available, and so easily worked, the continuance of simple conversion methods was encouraged. Even today many wood products are made in widely dispersed small factories reminiscent of cottage industries. The rapid development of a high and complex state of technology and the accompanying mechanization essential in converting iron to steel and usable consumer products were not as immediately essential to the continued widespread use of wood for buildings, vehicles, furniture, and the many other products.

A century ago the wood products used were either entire tree trunks or portions of the trunks. Whatever the final form of a wood product, whether a board or a violin, the internal structure of the material was always the same as that developed in the living tree. Only shape was changed. It is possible, but not necessarily economical, to produce boards or even the most intricate solid wood objects with only simple handtools. Products of solid wood, in the form of timber and lumber and the objects made from them, remain today the most important class of wood products. A certain degree of mechanization has been the key for producing better and more uniform wood products more efficiently than at any time in history. Thus, the products can meet the competition in today's marketplace.

The first, the slowest, and the most arduous task of the early wood craftsman was cutting logs into usable shapes and sizes. It is not surprising, then, that means for mechanizing this task were developed and adopted early in U.S. history. The basic process of producing lumber by forcing wood against a toothed cutting tool or moving the tool through the wood is still in use. Many important improvements, however, have been made. Utilization of the large West Coast logs triggered a great change in sawing equipment. Existing circular saws could not saw logs in excess of 4 feet in diameter with a desired accuracy; therefore, double circular saws cutting simultaneously from top and bottom were developed. Because of their size, these sawblades had to be excessively thick to prevent vibration while sawing. The resulting waste of material led to the development of a bandsaw. The bandsaw provided not only a relatively narrow saw kerf, the cut made by the saw, but also more accurate sawing.

Increased demand for fiber products brought about hydraulic and mechanical debarkers at sawmills so that barkfree chips suitable for pulping could be made from slabs and other residues of the sawmilling process. In 1950 the invention of the rotating ring debarker vastly increased the availability to the pulpmills of wood that could be chipped. Between 1963 and 1966 a chipping headrig was introduced at sawmills. In squaring a log for sawing, this headrig removes the outer material as chips rather than as slabs. This machine boosts lumber production per man-hour, increases the percentage of log converted to chips, and reduces sawdust.

Today's modern sawmill results from continuous progress; this includes development of new power sources and improved equipment for production, new methods for handling materials, and new equipment for drying and stacking lumber. These kinds of improvements have been aimed at rapid production of improved products with less waste. Similar progress has been made by the secondary wood industries that require lumber products as their source of raw material.

Forest operations of the lumbering industry are now largely mechanized. Efficient tractors have replaced teams of oxen and horses. Chain saws have replaced the backbreaking handsaws. Logs are moved to a mill by truck instead of by water or logging railroad. Mechanized handling and loading equipment has been developed; in some recent operations huge machines, like mammoth scissors, clip the tree at the base and remove the entire tree intact for further processing.

Within the last century new families of wood-based products have been developed that have profoundly affected wood utilization. These new products differ greatly from each other but have in common the principle of their manufacture. Wood reduced into pieces or fibers is reassembled into products, whose properties differ from those of the original material. Plywood, building boards of wood fibers or particles, and paper are examples. All are important in the U.S. economy and are now of particular interest for more efficient use of the wood resource.

Composite wood-based products cannot be made commercially with simple tools and equipment. Large capital investments are needed to supply the necessary equipment for handling materials, manufacturing, and quality control. These products and, in a sense, the industries that develop them are the result of research. Research has been and continues to be the pivotal base for both growth and product improvement.

A new trend has appeared recently in the industrialization of the forest products industries. Large industrial firms, sometimes called integrated industries, have developed to manufacture and market all types of wood products such as lumber, paper, plywood, and building boards. In log yards of these firms, each log can be channeled for its best and most efficient use. Waste from one product can be used as the raw material for another.

Plywood

A modern wood product developed during this century as an alternative and, in some ways an improvement to lumber, is plywood. It is made of thin layers of knife-cut wood, known as veneer. These are bonded together with adjacent veneers arranged so that their grains are at right angles. During the early part of this century plywood was made chiefly in the East from hardwoods such as yellow-poplar, sweetgum, birch, and walnut. Plywood was used for sewing machine cabinets, desk tops, doors, and furniture. Because of the animal and vegetable glues used at that time, plywood was restricted to interiors where it would remain dry and was not used for construction.

Douglas-fir plywood was introduced as a novelty at the Lewis and Clark Exposition held in Portland, Oregon, in 1905. A small Portland firm manufacturing veneer baskets and fruit containers had made the samples by laborious hand methods. A young college student, Tom Autzen, was assigned to manage the plywood exhibit. Autzen found so much interest in his display that he was motivated to pursue the plywood business and later became one of the leaders in a growing Douglas-fir plywood industry. Production did not begin to expand significantly until after World War I.

During World War I military needs for both lumber and hardwood plywood were great. Workers received training as wood procurement specialists and inspectors for the government. Lawrence Ottinger was among those sent to the Forest Products Laboratory in Madison, Wisconsin, to get training in wood inspection techniques. His teacher was Arthur Koehler, a scientist

Wood building panels find a ready market in the construction industry. Here insulating board is being used for wall sheathing and plywood for roof sheathing. (Photo by W. G. Youngquist)

who received much publicity for his detective work on the wood in the Lindberg kidnap ladder. Ottinger was a born salesman. At the end of the war he marketed wartime-surplus aircraft plywood, which he had purchased from the government at bargain prices. Being a visionary individual, he named his business the U.S. Plywood Company. This company flourished first in hardwood plywood manufacturing in the East, and later nationwide in softwood plywood, lumber, pulp and paper, and other forest products manufacturing and sales.

As in many industrial developments, success often awaits progress in related fields. Plywood required a good adhesive. It was not until 1935 that synthetic resin adhesives, complex products of a sophisticated chemical process, were considered for bonding plywood. These adhesives, so superior to natural glues, stimulated production of an "exterior" plywood for use in boats and in outdoor construction unprotected from the elements. The ruggedness of plywood bonded with synthetic resin glues was apparent by the late 1930s when a plywood boat made a mad dash down the turbulent Colorado River.

The reliability and versatility of the newer resin-glued plywood products made these materials important during World War II and led to a continued expansion of markets thereafter. About 20 billion square feet of plywood were produced in the United States in 1972.

Initially softwood construction plywood was made almost entirely of Douglas-fir. Southern yellow pine plywood came on the market for construction purposes in 1963 and currently accounts for about one quarter of the total production. Other western softwoods, such as western hemlock, the true firs, western larch, and Engelmann spruce, are also used.

Decorative plywood for wall paneling, cabinets, furniture, and many other products consists of native American species, such as walnut, cherry, oak, elm, and ash. Prior to 1950 native woods supplied these markets almost exclusively. A change in tariffs stimulated imports, and, since about 1950, a large percentage of the thin, prefinished wall paneling has been imported.

Building Boards of Wood Fibers or Particles

Building panels of reconstituted wood include insulation

*Vast quantities of wood are needed to supply America's paper needs.
(Courtesy U. S. Forest Service)*

Ease of handling, treatment to minimize decay losses, and improved inventory control has led to the storage of wood in chip instead of log form. (Courtesy Forest Prod. Lab.)

boards, hardboards, and particleboards. Building fiberboards, hardboards, and insulation boards are composed of interfelted wood fibers. Particleboards, also called chipcore, chipboard, or flakeboard, come from small chips or flakes of wood — planer shavings, sawdust, or specially made flakes — bonded with an adhesive. Leftovers from wood-using industries supply about 60 percent of the raw material for these reconstituted wood products. Although U.S. patents for different types of reconstituted wood date back more than 100 years, this type of panel is really a product of the 20th century.

Insulation board is the oldest type. Lightweight insulation boards have effective thermal and sound-insulating properties that usually dictate their use in construction. In recent years almost two-thirds of the houses in the United States with exterior sheathing have insulation board sheathing. Reconstituted wood panels make good acoustical ceiling tile, roof insulation and decking, and sound-deadening board in walls.

Hardboard, a hot-pressed fiberboard, sometimes has a binder added. The board generally is less than 1/2-inch thick. The largest market for hardboard is house siding either as large vertical panels or as horizontal lap siding. Other uses for hardboard include floor underlayment, prefinished wall paneling, and storage walls in a form known as pegboard.

The newest of the reconstituted wood products, particleboard, was first manufactured commercially in the United States about 1945. The industry has grown rapidly in the last 20 years. Production in 1955 was less than 200 million square feet, on a 3/8-inch thickness basis. Now annual production has reached about 6 billion square feet.

The first use for particleboard in this country was as corestock in furniture, still one of its leading markets. About one-third of all particleboard is made for floor underlayment. Also, more than 90 percent of the single-width mobile homes have particleboard floor decking. Some exterior grades of particleboard are promoted as house siding and sheathing. The increasing markets for reconstituted wood materials in the construction industry promote the more efficient use of the U.S. wood resource.

Paper

Paralleling but contrasting the slow industrialization and

technological improvements in the sawmilling industry during the early part of the last century has been a spectacular development of a pulp and paper industry based on wood fiber. About the middle of the 19th century, the demand for paper surpassed the available supplies of rags then used almost universally. The long fibers of spruce wood, obtained by grinding this wood, served well in producing paper. The manufacture of paper from woodpulp became a new industry that required new equipment with heavy power demand and large capital investments. From the beginning survival of the industry depended on aggressive industrialization to meet a steadily increasing demand. The consumption of pulpwood for paper and paperboard has risen from 6 million cords in 1925 to more than 77 million cords in 1974. U.S. per capita consumption of paper and paper products in 1976 was 589 pounds, the highest in the world. More than nine-tenths of today's paper comes from wood pulp. Paper, an indispensable commodity today, re-emphasizes America's dependence on forests.

Of three major commercially feasible methods of converting wood into paper pulp, the first was the mechanical or groundwood process of grinding wood into a fibrous slurry. This process has the advantage of converting almost 100 percent of wood into pulp. Two other processes were introduced early in the 20th century. The sulfate, or kraft process, originated in Germany in 1884. It was first applied commercially in this country in 1909 at a mill in Roanoke Rapids, South Carolina. The most recently introduced major pulping process, the semichemical that combines the mechanical and the chemical fiber-separating forces, was developed at the Forest Products Laboratory, Madison, Wisconsin, in 1922. It was first used commercially in 1925 at Knoxville, Tennessee.

During the last 50 years, technical advances have been achieved in all phases of pulpmill and papermill operations that include the following: improved harvesting equipment and, recently, whole-tree harvesting; outside storage and pneumatic handling of chips; adoption of the kraft pulping process (now 70% of all pulping) with chemical recovery, odor suppression, continuous digesters, and computer control; wider paper machines with twinwire sheet formers that produce products of greater uniformity faster; and reduction of stream and air pollution.

A change in the paper industry over the past 50 years that

has also required new equipment and new processes is the increasing use of hardwoods along with the softwoods, spruces, pines, and hemlocks, which had been preferred. Today, hardwoods furnish about a fourth of the pulpwood cut in the United States, and the proportion is expected to increase to 40 percent by the end of this century. Hardwoods have become an indispensable source of fiber for many grades of paper.

The expansion of pulpwood materials to include almost all of the U.S. wood species has brought a geographical expansion of the pulp industry. Large mills using the most advanced techniques have been established near old hardwood forests and in areas where cutover softwood forests have been replaced by hardwoods. The center of the industry remains in the South, where it moved in the 1930s when development of the kraft process allowed the use of the resinous southern pines. Southern pines supply half of the the total volume of pulpwood.

Wood Products Research

Technological improvements during the past century have brought greater production efficiency to the industry. At the same time they have brought wood products with better performance and improved serviceability to the consumer. As in all industry, most technological improvements are based on research.

President Theodore Roosevelt was instrumental in the creation of the National Forest System and the U. S. Forest Service that administers it. In 1902 he summed up the sentiment of the leading conservationists in the phrase: "Forestry is the conservation of forests through wise use." Leaders of wood products industries including manufacturers of such diverse products as lumber, furniture, pulp and paper, wagons and wagon wheels, caskets, barrels and boxes, flooring, trunks, and pianos, declared themselves united in support of conservation-oriented research at a central Forest Products Laboratory. In 1906 they met in Washington to adopt a resolution that is as meaningful today as it was 70 years ago:

> Wood is an essential material in every industry. Nearly all forms of wood are rapidly rising in price, on account of the diminished supply and the great demand. This laboratory would lead the way on one hand to making available a

greater supply, and on the other to increasing the duration of timber in service. It would, therefore, affect favorably both supply and demand and, in consequence, be an institution for the benefit of the entire public.[1]

With strong support of foresters and conservationists, the U. S Forest Service established the Forest Products Laboratory in 1910 at Madison, Wisconsin, in cooperation with the University of Wisconsin. Since that date the Laboratory has been the center of wood utilization research for the United States and has provided leadership for similar research efforts throughout the United States and in other countries.

In addition to the Forest Products Laboratory, forest products research is also conducted at industry, association, private, state, and university laboratories. The research is frequently coordinated between laboratories working on specific problems. Important findings have led to improved wood utilization. Assigning credit for specific achievements to an individual or a single laboratory is almost impossible. Alexander Graham Bell observed that great discoveries and improvements invariably involve the cooperation of many minds.

The early emphasis on conservation through wise use is even more meaningful today than in 1910, since today the world-wide shortages of materials of all kinds confront us, especially the nonrenewable resources of petroleum and minerals. At the same time concerns for energy conservation and pollution reduction have become acute. Interest continues to focus on wood because of its renewability, low energy requirements in conversion, recycleability, and low polluting side effects. The need for research to exploit all of wood's potential benefits continues unabated.

Fortunately research in unrelated fields, where progress may have advanced more rapidly to meet the needs of military or space technologists, may be drawn upon and adapted to the needs of wood processors. This can be illustrated by a sawmilling example. Lumber mills have the problem of producing rectangular lumber items of specified sizes from cylindrical logs. Lumber yield is, therefore, complicated by the need to fit rectangles into a circle. Slight variations in location of a saw line can result in substantial differences in lumber yield. The crucial step is the first or opening cut, because the resulting face, or saw line, fixes the position of subsequent cuts in parallel planes.

Research facilities of the Forest Products Laboratory of the U.S. Forest Service in Madison, Wisconsin (aerial view below). Strong support by both industry and conservationists brought about the establishment of this center for wood products research in 1910. (Courtesy Forest Prod. Lab.)

To solve the problem of the first cut, sawing systems using computerized, automatic equipment were developed in the early 1970s. Automatic diameter-measuring devices relay information to a minicomputer, programed to handle various options and variables. The computer selects the best sawing pattern for the log and directs precision-built saw, carriage, and setworks to cut the log in the selected pattern. These systems, which are rapidly being adopted, have introduced an era of sophistication not previously experienced by the industry. In addition improvement in volume yields can range from 10 to 90 percent depending on the log diameters being sawed.

Early in the century the monumental task was begun of determining strength and other physical properties of commercial woods from trees grown in the United States. Because trees are products of nature, no two trees in a forest, although of the same species, are exactly alike. Wood properties vary from tree to tree and even from board to adjacent board. The infinite variety of wood material nature provides is a pleasant challenge to a fine craftsman but is a hindrance to a designer who must be concerned for the safety of a structure.

Scientific sampling and test methods were developed first; then a qualitative evaluation of the forest resource was begun. This information made it possible to segregate wood material into a number of visual grades and to assign design values to the grades. With a greater efficiency of materials, designers can now choose a species of wood that best meets their needs. Creativity in design can be executed with confidence. The scientific information now available on wood made possible the development of modern standards for the production and the use of wood products.

In earlier times wood products were made and used locally. The pioneers frequently selected trees from the forest and fashioned their own products. If there was need to purchase material, brief verbal or written instructions were sufficient. As distance between wood supplier and user increased and as transportation improved, the person-to-person arrangement no longer sufficed for purchasing wood materials. Instructions and requirements became more detailed. With time they have been developed into standardized rules and regulations.

Today wood and wood products are marketed nationally and internationally. The development of realistic and universally accepted product codes and standards that govern product sizes, tolerances, appearance, strength properties, and often performance make this possible. The development of workable standards for wood products made from a diverse product of nature is of major significance in the more efficient use of the U.S. timber resource.

Research has been the impetus for bringing many new wood products into existence. Exterior plywoods, laminated beams, and structural building boards depend on adhesive bonding as an essential to their functional performance. These types of products, or at least some applications of them, would not have been possible without the significant advancements in adhesive technology in recent years.

Early glues, such as animal-and-hide glues, were developed from materials of natural origin. Casein, also an animal product, and vegetable proteins later formed the base for adhesives, and are still used to some extent. All of these types, however, lack resistance to moisture and to fungi; thus, products that incorporate them are limited in use.

The greatest advances in adhesives have come since the midthirties with various coal tar- or petroleum-based synthetic resin adhesive systems developed to meet specific needs. Some of these adhesive systems have been shown to produce bonds stronger and more durable than the bond of the wood cells. Polyvinyl resin emulsion adhesives, the commonly used white glues, have largely replaced animal glues in the furniture industry for edge-bonding and assembly operations.

Another crucial advance in wood use brought about by research is the development of effective preservative treatments. Early pioneers soon learned that some of the native species resisted decay much better than did others. Whenever possible they selected cedar, baldcypress, chestnut, locust, white oak, or other decay-resistant species for use in fenceposts or in other situations in which the wood would be in contact with the ground. Some of the early settlers in the Midwest brought locust saplings with them from the East to assure themselves of a future supply of durable fenceposts.

Preservative treatments have made possible extended service life of all wood species used in unfavorable conditions. The treatment is essentially an impregnation of a wood with a water-

or an oil-borne toxic, which prevents or retards wood attack by biological organisms. Among the great variety of products customarily treated with preservatives are utility poles, marine piling, fenceposts, railroad ties, lumber, timber, and plywood. Treatment imparts a service life 10 to 20 times that of these wood products with no treatment. The prolonged endurance of treated wood results in annual savings of about 2.3 billion cubic feet of wood, one-sixth that of present consumption.

Users of the U.S. wood resource today consume about 13.7 billion cubic feet yearly. Some of the early wood uses, such as for masts, ships, plank roads, wagons, and even for fuel, are of little or no importance today. Wood, however, has retained many of its traditional uses—for housing, industrial buildings, furniture, and utility poles. A great many new uses have been added. Wood today is sometimes so greatly modified in the manufacturing process that even an expert cannot identify a product as having a wood base.

Wood for Housing

A panorama of the American landscape shows how succeeding generations met the housing challenge. In both rural and urban areas the old and the new, the pretentious and the humble, stand side by side for comparison. Each residential structure reflects economic constraints, availability of materials, state of architecture, and often, the specific needs and wishes of the owner. Current home builders face the new challenge of material and energy conservation.

Wood has retained its essential role in housing which provides the largest single market for lumber, plywood, and a wide variety of other wood products. About a third of U.S. softwood lumber and plywood produced goes into new housing. So does substantial volumes of other timber products, such as hardwood, plywood, particleboard, and insulation board. The 1.9 million living units constructed in 1970 required a staggering 12.3 billion board feet of lumber, 6.3 billion square feet of plywood, and 2 billion square feet of hardboard, insulation board, and particleboard.

Despite technological developments, the first half of the 20th century brought few changes in residential architecture. The two-story house with white clapboard siding remained the most popular style until the arrival, after World War II, of the low-

Wood has retained its essential role in housing. (Photo by W. G. Youngquist)

The low profile ranchhouse, a popular native new architecture, emphasizes the natural appearance of wood. (Courtesy Gunard Hans, architect, Forest Prod. Lab.)

profile ranchhouse. A native new wood architecture that emphasized use of the natural appearance of wood began on the West Coast. In a few years it became the widespread new image of the American home.

The basic light-frame construction system widely employed today is a native development with relatively few basic changes since its introduction in the mid-1830s in Chicago. The balloon-frame construction system gradually developed into the combination-frame and then the platform-frame to minimize the effects of wood shrinkage. The customary 16-inch spacing of studs and joists, which had become established practice by the 1850s, remained essentially unchanged for over a century until the more economical 24-inch spacing, permitted by improved lumber grading and production practices, became generally recognized by the building codes.

Widespread use of building insulation and panel materials, such as fiberboard sheathing and plywood subflooring, largely replaced lower grade boards in house construction after the depression. The ranch house made natural redwood and cedar siding the most popular exterior finish, thus further reducing the use of other woods once favored for siding. While the availability of plywood paneling has made wood grains more popular for wall surfaces, composition flooring and carpeting have largely re-placed once cherished hardwood floors. Wood decks of naturally decay resistant or pressure-treated lumber have replaced the screened porches once so popular.

Builders of houses, low rise residential apartments, and commercial buildings quickly recognized the advantages of panel materials as they became available. Sheets, usually 4 feet by 8 feet, are relatively lightweight and easy to handle, easy to apply, and provide strength and rigidity not formerly attainable in light frame construction. Thus, a structure can be enclosed against the elements in record time.

As a result of new and improved building code requirements, the construction standards for light-frame wood houses have reached a high degree of uniformity throughout the country. Regional variations still exist in other construction types. The post-and-beam timber frame has retained its popularity in New England, as has the log cabin in the western states. A pole-type building system has been developed for the sloping hillside sites

Prototype prefabricated houses were erected on the grounds of the Forest Products Laboratory in 1937. Eleanor Roosevelt visited these homes and expressed great interest in the possibilities of this building method for improving America's housing situation. (Courtesy Forest Prod. Lab.)

in California, and adobe is still popular in the southwestern states.

In recent years the housing industry has adopted new products, prefabricated components, and new construction techniques. Although outwardly houses have changed little, important advances have resulted from the use of improved materials and construction methods. Trussed roof rafters with metal connector plates were introduced in the 1950s and now, less than 25 years later, they are used in close to 75 percent of all new single-family homes. Similarly constructed wood floor trusses were introduced in the early 1970s, and already are found in more than 10 percent of all multi-family buildings.

Although the possibilities in prefabrication had been tested as early as the California gold rush of 1848, when large quantities of precut lumber were shipped around the Cape, prefabrication on a large scale did not develop until nearly 100 years later. The stressed-skin concept introduced by the Forest Products Laboratory in the 1930s permitted efficient factory production of insulated modular lightweight plywood wall panels with wood ribs. In 1937 two prototype houses using this panel system were erected on the Laboratory grounds. In the fall of that year Eleanor Roosevelt visited these houses and expressed great interest in the possibilities of this building method for improving America's housing situation. One of these houses, in excellent condition, still stands on the Laboratory grounds. The other was dismantled after 29 years of service; the components were structurally evaluated and found still fully serviceable. By 1939 some 700 houses using this system in whole or in part had been erected in the United States by one company alone. The manufacture of house components for assembly on site and the manufacture of fully factory built homes is now a major and nationwide industry.

The use of pneumatic hammers and staplers and fully automated panel and truss assembly lines has permitted significant savings in labor cost without a reduction in the quality of the finished product. The housing industry has found prefabrication a good tool for control of construction costs in an inflationary market. The use of prefabricated assemblies and prefinished materials permits better quality control, minimizing the possibility of production irregularities due to inclement weather and human errors.

The rehabilitation of structurally sound older homes to bring them up to present day living standards is gaining rapid acceptance. The movement goes far beyond a nostalgic return to yesteryear. Many older homes are being structurally modified to meet new needs and insulated to conserve energy at a fraction of the cost of a comparable new home. The savings in material is of special significance now.

Wood for Nonresidential Construction

Almost 10 percent of the lumber and plywood used in the United States in 1970 and large quantities of building boards were used in constructing large structures such as offices, stores, warehouses, schools, hospitals, and highway bridges. Many are of conventional design, but new materials and standardized wood products with known design properties have resulted in better than conventional structures and in new architectural opportunities.

Laminated structural lumber—the result of gluing together layers of lumber with all grains essentially parallel into large shapes to meet specific design requirements—has gained wide acceptance. Because of their attractiveness, wood structural members are usually left exposed to lend natural aesthetic qualities to the design. The development of waterproof adhesives makes possible the use of laminated beams in outdoor exposures. The graceful aesthetic effects of laminated arches have won them a place in many churches and public buildings. The large clear spans that can be achieved, many over 250 feet, are also ideal for aircraft hangars and sports arenas. A dramatic example of the use of laminated and solid wood is the Keystone Wye interchange on U.S. Highway 16 near Mount Rushmore, South Dakota. Wood was chosen to blend its natural beauty with the surrounding landscape. This trilevel interchange has a 290-foot-long upper bridge supported by 155-foot-long arches over a lower bridge.

Wood in Transportation and Communications

Throughout most of American history, travel, if not by foot or horseback, was by a wood conveyance—canoe, ship, coach, or railroad passenger car. The drastic changes in transportation

The manufacture of factory built homes is now a nationwide industry. Complete floor, wall, and roof sections (above) are being built for truck delivery and assembly on site (below). (Courtesy Wausau Homes, Inc., Wausau, Wis.)

These two homes were factory manufactured and erected on site. (Courtesy Wausau Homes, Inc., Wausau, Wis.)

This footbridge, a three-span glulam arch, is an integral part of the golf course at Wentworth-by-the-Sea, a resort located in Newcastle, New Hampshire. Maurice Witmer, architect/engineer. (Courtesy American Institute of Timber Construction)

The functional and beautiful Keystone Wye traffic interchange is located on U.S. Highway 16 near Mount Rushmore, South Dakota. The upper laminated wood arches are 155 feet in length. (Courtesy South Dakota Highway Dept.)

Graceful laminated arches curve up to join at the highest point of the ceiling at St. Martin's Academy, Rapid City, South Dakota. (Courtesy American Institute of Timber Construction)

during the past 100 years made wood a specialized rather than a customary basic material for modern conveyances. In the 20th century wartime steel shortages and strategic requirements brought about several wood shipbuilding revivals. During World War I on both coasts, wood ships were constructed for commercial firms and for the Navy. World War II brought another revival. In 1944, for instance, the Navy required 9 million tons of steel and 3 million tons of wood for its construction program.[2]

In railroading wood has lost little of its traditional importance. Wood is still used for tracks, cars, bridges, stations, fences, snowsheds, tunnel linings, docks, wharves, bulkheads, crossing planks, and dams. Treating ties with preservatives began early in the 1900s. Today ties must be replaced only one-third as often as they were at the turn of the century. Indicative of the declining importance of railroads, however, is a drop in annual production of railroad ties—from 96 million in the 1920s to 21 million in 1970.

Largely forgotten is the fact that early aircraft, including those used in World War I, were made of wood. Wood wing spars and ribs were used to support fabric covering. This type of construction continued through and after World War II for lightweight, inexpensive private planes and civilian trainers. Between the two wars, plywood was introduced as a covering for spars and framing on wings and fuselages of military trainers and in the faster, more expensive private planes. At the beginning of World War II, American military and commercial planes were almost entirely of metal, but primary and advanced trainers and gliders made use of wood and plywood. Shortages of metals early in the war brought about an increased use of wood in aircraft, and led to the development of molded plywood construction in varying thicknesses and complex shapes. Production of wood trainers and gliders accelerated rapidly, and new designs in wood construction appeared. The most publicized wood aircraft, flown just once in 1947, was a "flying boat" by Howard Hughes. Built mainly from molded birch plywood, the aircraft construction was an engineering breakthrough.

Communication breakthroughs also led to more uses for wood and wood products. In 1884 Samuel Morse drew up a specification for procuring 700 straight and sound chestnut poles to carry new telegraph wires. At the Philadelphia Centennial Exhibition in 1876 Alexander Graham Bell exhibited his newly invented telephone, thus creating a new demand for wood poles. By the 1920s almost 2 million wood poles were required annually for U.S. communications systems. Some authorities predicted the supply would run out. But for the last 25 years, the United States has produced and used 5 or 6 million wood poles annually. Chestnut was originally the predominant species for utility poles; about 50 years ago it was cedar, primarily northern cedar. Today 85 percent of the poles are of southern pine (small poles), the remaining of western redcedar and Douglas-fir (large poles). Since 1930 virtually all utility poles have been treated with preservatives. In the last few decades some large transmission structures have been made of glued-laminated members.

Wood in Shipping and Handling

Wood is not only a major source of industrial products. In the form of the familiar corrugated fiberboard container it is the means by which most industrial and agricultural products are now shipped. During the last 50 years, wood fiberboard has replaced solid wood as the predominant shipping container material. Corrugated fiberboard containers are remarkably versatile, lightweight, and adaptable for all kinds of products. This material not only provides ample protection, but also lends itself to automatic setup, filling, closing, sealing, handling, and inventory control. Its impact on the environment is minimal, since it is reusable, biodegradable, and easily recycled. More than 200 billion square feet of fiberboard were used for containers in the United States in 1972. Many of the fiberboard containers are shipped in groups on wood pallets, which reduce individual handling and allow forklift trucks to be used. This results in increased efficiency and decreased product damage. The pallet industry, only 30 years old, has grown rapidly, and in 1974 produced 205 million shipping pallets.

Wood for Furniture

Furniture, so intimately associated with daily living and personal uses, remains an ever present reminder of the usefulness, durability and beauty of wood. Because of the wide use of wood for furniture, the merits and beauty of various wood species and the

Beautifully grained, wood cabinet (above) makes functional storage spaces in all areas of the home. (Courtesy Baker Furniture Inc., Holland, Mich.) In modern kitchens (below) the "Hoosier" cabinet and pantry shelves have given way to built-in cabinets, shelves, and counters. (Courtesy Kitchen Mart, Madison, Wis.)

best finishing and upkeep methods are often debated. Furniture also provides an important and visible tie to the past. Almost every family possesses an heirloom chair, table, or other piece of wood furniture. The search for antique furniture, which began more than a century ago, continues with increasing vigor.

The well-founded tradition in favor of wood furniture remains. The furniture industry, a major consumer of lumber, uses annually between 2 and 2.5 billion board feet of the hardwoods and almost 1 billion board feet of the softwoods. Large quantities of the reconstituted wood products, hardboard and particleboards, are also used. Most of the wood comes from domestic species. Since no single species dominates the furniture market, the major part of the market is shared by 8 to 10 woods that include oak, pine, maple, pecan, walnut, cherry, and birch.

Important changes in furniture technology have been adopted in the last few years, especially the introduction of new adhesives. The development of specialized woodworking machinery for furniture manufacture has been marked by gradual improvements rather than the revolutionary breakthroughs. The notable inventions which have affected the furniture industry include the wide belt sander, automated tape controlled router, automatic edge sander, and the short cycle press. Modern manufacturing methods have brought good furniture within the price range of all. Many furniture manufacturers, however, believe their product does not lend itself to automation and have continued to employ single purpose machines.

Preferences in style change rapidly and are dependent on regional preferences. Furniture styles developed in colonial days still have a strong influence on present day furniture design. A few skilled craftsmen still produce hand crafted furniture comparable to that produced in colonial days. In general, however, the present trend is a rejection of elaborate and exotic designs in favor of natural or simplified forms. Interest grows in "country look" furniture of thick lumber, and all-wood furniture devoid of plastic decoration is preferred. The use of wood for the construction of "built-in" furniture, especially for kitchens, is rapidly increasing.

Chemicals from Wood

Production of chemicals from wood is not new. The chemicals

grouped under the general name "naval stores" still make up the most important chemicals derived from wood. The southern pines are the main source of these stores. The old methods of tree tapping for gum rosin and turpentine and extracting wood rosin and turpentine from dead logs and stumps are still practiced. However, their share in the production of naval stores has been steadily declining. This is giving way to extracting naval stores as a byproduct (tall oil) of the kraft production of paper pulp.

About 1.2 billion pounds of crude tall oil are now produced annually in the United States. By distillation, tall oil yields rosin and fatty acids. These chemicals are used in manufacturing many useful products that include adhesives, asphalt tile, carbon paper, detergents, gasoline additives, lubricants, varnishes, pine oil disinfectants, printing inks, soaps, vinyl plasticizers, and water-proofing agents.

Naval stores are among the so-called extractives or nonwood substances that occur in wood and range to up to 10 percent of wood weight. Smaller amounts of chemicals are derived from chemical decomposition of the three basic constitutents of wood substance: cellulose, hemicellulose, and lignin. For instance, pulping processes, which obtain a cellulose-rich substance suitable for papermaking, leave as byproducts the so-called spent liquors, which contain carbohydrate and lignate decomposition products. These may be fermented into industrial ethyl alcohol and, by various other processes, made into yeast suitable for animal and poultry feed and vanillin flavoring. The spent liquors from kraft pulping are mostly concentrated and used as fuel. A portion, however, helps in the production of dimethyl sulfoxide, a very useful solvent. The rapidly increasing price of petroleum, the source of many industrial chemicals, has stimulated renewed interest in deriving still more organic chemicals from wood.

Wood as Fuel

Use of wood for fuel, one of its oldest uses, continues in the United States, although the proportion of roundwood harvested for fuel is less than five percent of the total. In other parts of the world 50 percent of the wood harvested is used for fuel. In 1970, U.S. fuelwood consumption was 1.4 billion cubic feet. This included about 314 million cubic feet of roundwood from growing

Exquisite wood bowls are turned from hardwood burls by master craftsman Harry Nohr of Mineral Point, Wisconsin. Burls, woody outgrowths on a tree, occur where a cluster of buds arise in other than the normal position. (Courtesy Mrs. Harry Nohr)

The Dancer. *Laminated mahogany (left).* Sculptor. *Cedar (right). From the book* Arnold Flaten, Sculptor, *Augsburg Publishing House. (Photo by Orin M. Lofthus)*

trees, 225 million cubic feet from other sources such as dead and discarded timber, and 723 million cubic feet from residues of wood-processing plants.

Charcoal briquets fuel barbecue ovens in millions of backyards across the country. They are made from sawmill residue such as slabs, sawdust, bark, and some low-quality roundwood. The charcoal industry produces 600,000 tons of charcoal briquets annually from about 1.8 million tons of wood, the equivalent of 120 million additional cubic feet of fuelwood.

In addition to ordinary logs, fireplace-size logs produced from sawdust, shavings, and other finely divided residue have become popular. More than 40 million of these logs are produced annually.

Most of the remaining wood residue used as fuel is burned for heat and for steampower in mills and wood-processing plants. The pulp and paper industry, the fourth largest energy consumer in the United States, consumes the largest amount of wood residue for fuel. It derives 10 percent of its energy from wood residues and an additional 32 percent from combustion of wood-derived materials in spent pulping liquors.

Miscellaneous Uses of Wood

Wood is no longer the universally used material of 200 years ago. Much of the woodenware hand-made by early settlers has no modern descendants or has been replaced by metal, glass, or plastic. Yet a great many wood items are still familiar objects in every household: rolling pins, mashers, chopping boards, bowls, utensil holders, trays, boxes, clothespins, and baskets. Kitchen knives and axes, rakes, shovels, and other tools still commonly have wood handles, as do brooms, hairbrushes, paintbrushes, and artist's brushes. Wood cribs and chests are still customary, and wood is still used in ladders, shingles, fencing, and in many farm structures.

Most of the small wood manufactures that flourished 100 years ago thrive today, including wood spools, matchsticks, pencils, pipes, rulers, baseball bats, toys, picture and mirror frames, models, musical instruments, caskets, and clockcases. Wood barrels are still required for wine and whiskey and are being revived for some dry goods. Although this may be considered a minor use of wood, 215 million board feet of lumber were used for barrels in 1970[3].

Other uses of wood are reviving through a renaissance of handicrafts in the United States. Thirty years ago woodworkers and individual furnituremakers, survivors of a great tradition, were few in number. There was no place to study crafts and no apprentice system as in Europe. After World War II, however, there was an influx of European craftsmen, many offering to teach. Schools and universities began to adopt crafts programs. Most of today's young craftsmen are university trained. They grow in number as more people discover the satisfaction of handworking natural, organic materials. Many imaginative amateur architects are building their own houses out of wood. Communities of craftsmen have emerged throughout the country, and handmade wood furniture, boats, baskets, toys, and utensils are appearing. The products are not only useful and of high quality but can be beautiful works of art as well.

Wood, as an artistic material, has never lost its vitality. Wood sculpture — religious objects, portraiture, and animal carvings — is still a major folk art. Wood engravings and woodcuts have continued to grow in popularity among professional artists; the prints are in effect multiple original works of art. Wood engravings have begun to appear again as illustrations in serious novels and other types of books. Americans are becoming increasingly aware of the need to use the renewable resource of wood and to adapt it to a modern technology. With this awareness, craftsmen and artists, undoubtedly, will insure the preservation of the intimate knowledge and high standards of workmanship of wood, a part of the oldest heritage of this nation.

Wood — The Renewable Resource

Since wood is so essential to the economy and is so universally used, reliable information on timber supplies and predicted demands for timber increase in importance. Yet a comparison of the periodic major reports of the U.S. timber situation may cause only confusion for anyone unfamiliar with the methods of measuring, inventorying, and using timber. Only one theme will be found consistent throughout the various

Pilot scale demonstration plant in Madison, Wisconsin, recovers useful wood fibers and particles from mixed urban trash. In a joint research venture the City of Madison and the Forest Products Laboratory have shown that significant quantities of useable fibers and particles can be obtained by mechanical separation. The process awaits full scale implementation. (Courtesy Forest Prod. Lab.)

Problem or opportunity? Piles of urban wood trash such as this pollute the landscape all across America. However, the technology already exists for turning this waste into thousands of useful products such as this book paper. (Courtesy Photography Northwest, Portland, Ore.)

inventory documents of the 20th century: a concern that the much dreaded and often predicted timber famine is likely to arrive in the near future.

For the greater part of the two centuries of this nation's existence, timber was considered an inexhaustible resource. Our superb virgin timber stands plus fertile soil, rich supplies of minerals, and hard-working people made America into a rich and prosperous land. Today, no virgin timber remains to be exploited. The virgin hardwoods, spruce, and pine of the Northeast as well as the virgin pine and oak timber of the South have been exhausted. The magnificent white pine stands of the northern Lake States were harvested in a relatively short period about the turn of this century. More recently, the large industrial timber establishments, propelled by World War II and the booming economy that followed, have almost depleted the virgin timber of the West. Most forested land has experienced the logger's ax for a second and even a third time. The timber famine would indeed be here if wood, like minerals, could be utterly depleted.

The miracle of wood is that nature has made it renewable. The miracle is so astounding even America's early foresters failed to appreciate the potential of the forest land to reproduce timber crops. Early foresters consistently predicted imminent shortages. Only in recent years, because the backlog of virgin timber has essentially been consumed, has the forester's role as a manager of timber crops begun to be appreciated. As a result some foresters now confidently predict that U.S. forests have potential to provide a reasonable quantity of forest products for more than 400 million people.

Progress in avoiding the long-predicted timber famine cannot be attributed solely to nature and to foresters manipulating the forces of nature. A most important element for progress is improving the utilization habits of wood processors. Early loggers, highly selective in their harvesting methods, chose only the biggest and the very best trees for the sawmill. The remaining trees were left in the forest: small trees, trees of undesirable form, partially decayed trees, dead trees, and a whole group of "less desirable species." The harvesting process itself wasted even the highest quality trees. Large portions of each tree were left as high stumps, limby wood, and broken logs.

Traditionally foresters have accepted industry's evaluation of

Logs are now moved to waiting trucks by efficient mechanized equipment. (Courtesy Weyerhaeuser Company, Tacoma, Wash.)

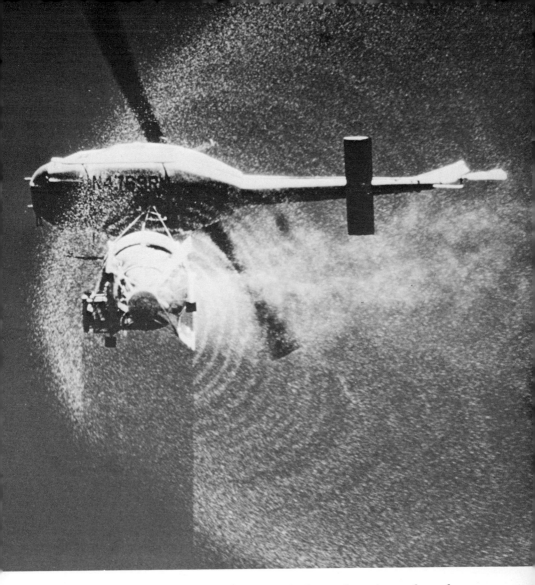

Fertilizing a future forest on difficult terrain is much easier and much more economical with the aid of a helicopter. (Courtesy Weyerhaeuser Company, Tacoma, Wash.)

what is usable at a mill. That appraisal, in turn, was influenced by visions of limitless supplies of inexpensive timber. Inventories of the nation's timber supplies are based not on volume but on industry's conversion practices. For example the "board foot" exists as a measure of standing timber in the United States instead of cubic volume used elsewhere in the world.

Efficient Utilization Opportunities

Perhaps one of the most dramatic illustrations of utilization improvement in recent years comes from one of the largest of the nation's timber firms. In 1948 a typical acre of Douglas-fir timberland harvested by that company produced logs that were sawed into 3,640 cubic feet of lumber, while 14,280 cubic feet of wood were left as waste or were used as fuel. A quarter of a century later in 1972, a typical acre of Douglas-fir timberland harvested produced 3,248 cubic feet of lumber. In addition, from that same acre the company produced 1,272 cubic feet of plywood, 1,026 cubic feet of particleboard, 2,234 cubic feet of linerboard (a heavy paper product for containers), and 6,341 cubic feet of saleable chips and logs. The total yield of products amounted to 14,121 cubic feet! Only 3,247 cubic feet of wood were left at the mill for fuel or were wasted[4]. This is a magnificent achievement in utilization efficiency, and yet it may be assumed that improvement is not yet at an end!

To arrive at production statistics to predict future timber demand and supply, it is understandable that customarily a conservative position has been adopted. Perhaps this has been influenced by the early "low technology" image of the timber industries. Thus, Forest Service predictions assumed that technological improvements in the lumber industry would lead to increases of 2 to 4 percent per decade in product output from a given volume of roundwood. A most recent estimate of utilization improvements from technological change, based on a study of timber input and product output from World War II to the present, indicates an average advance of 1.75 percent per year — almost 20 percent in a decade[5]. The 20 percent deals only with utilization efficiency at the processing plant, and does not include harvesting gains similar to those of the Douglas-fir example cited above.

In 1970 the U.S. Forest Service estimated the United States

used approximately 45 billion board feet of softwood sawtimber and 11 billion board feet of hardwood sawtimber from forests. By the year 2000 demands for domestic softwood supplies are expected to increase to 54 billion board feet; those for hardwood, to 21 billion. If these figures prove correct, assuming little or no progress in forestry improvement, the United States forests would indeed be nearing depletion by the year 2000. Timber would be cut faster than grown.

Much can occur to upset predictions. Prices will inevitably rise, and demand and supply will reach a new balance. Continuing research and its implementation can be expected to bring about great improvements in growing timber and in developing more efficient methods for timber use. Because of the growing shortages of nonrenewable resources on which a high standard of living depends, the challenge of attaining improvements in the availability and the use of wood daily becomes more urgent.

Much more could be said about the status of the U.S. timber inventory. For example, the bulk of softwood, now the mainstay of the industry, lies in the West. Inventories there diminish at rates that overshadow the gains being made in the East where there is an overabundance of hardwoods. For the nation as a whole, the present balance between growth and removal, regardless of species, is favorable. Furthermore, the net annual growth of timber is rising, although still only about one-half the potential of fully stocked stands. More timber is harvested for sawing into lumber than for all other products combined. Pulpwood accounts for about one-third of all roundwood products from U.S. forests. Within a relatively few years the problem is likely to be a shortage of softwood sawtimber and will require a major readjustment in wood-use patterns.

Conservation and Forest Management Opportunities

Within the United States a number of underused or unused sources of wood fiber still remain. Recycling wood fiber products, mostly in the form of paperboard containers and to a lesser extent newspapers, is still at a relatively low level. Only about 20 percent of once-used paper products is recycled. In some parts of Europe and in Japan 50 percent is recycled. Economic incentives to

Only recently has the forester's role as manager of timber crops begun to be appreciated. (Courtesy Weyerhaeuser Company, Tacoma, Wash.)

greater recycling may be lacking at present, but the technology exists. It is inevitable that a high rate of recycling of once-used wood products will become reality.

A source of wood fiber, although not used, is the urban renewal waste from the demolition of old buildings. The reuse of once-used ties, timbers, pallets, and other large volume items could considerably relieve demands for additional timber from U.S. forests. Obviously the great variety in shapes, sizes, and qualities of wood products entering the recycling stream will be suitable mainly for recovery of wood fiber.

Some pulp experts predict the U.S. pulp industry will be able to exist entirely on wood residues from other wood-using industries, such as sawmills and plywood plants, from recycled wood fiber, and from solid wood objects. Added to all these sources will be ornamental and shade trees from urban parks and streets, a source of wood fiber not used that adds to the disposal problems of urban solid-waste handlers.

Utilization practices have obviously undergone vast transformations to adapt to the changes in available timber qualities and quantities. A nationwide need exists to exploit to the fullest the forestry opportunities for growing timber as a crop in an ever-increasing quantity. Already this has been accomplished for annual agricultural crops. Because of the long timespan required for growing trees, the problem is complex, and governmental agencies will have to assume responsibility for long-range planning.

Only a fraction of commercial timberland in the United States is operated as cropland with efficient husbandry. Industrial firms own about 14 percent of the country's most productive forest land and have taken aggressive forestry action to grow timber in increasing quantity and of improved quality. Twenty-seven percent of the commercial timberland is in government ownership — federal, state, county, and municipal — and this includes some of the less productive areas. Often care is purely custodial. Well over 50 percent of the most productive commercial land is owned by farmers and by a miscellany of small private ownerships. The quality of forest management practiced on this large segment of land varies greatly with each owner's interests and capabilities. Great opportunities exist for improvement of this segment.

The task of extending U.S. timber supplies and products to

accommodate the next century's needs has hardly begun. The need is great to put the 500 million acres of America's commercial forest land to work growing wood as a crop. The growing will require all of the innovations, the ingenuity, and the new developments from research that American scientists and professional forests can supply.

Americans have cause to be concerned about their future. America has completed a full cycle in the exploitation of the rich resources so abundant and important in making this nation a world power. Material resources and energy for industry are no longer readily available, and future supplies of both are expected to be critical. Of the major materials available for industry and for construction, only renewable wood is capable of serving our needs in perpetuity.

Plans are under way to approach the problems of renewable forest resources in a forthright and comprehensive manner. Federal legislation has initiated the Forest and Rangeland Renewable Resources Planning Act of 1974 to attack the overall problems of assessing the nation's renewable natural resources and of developing long-range policies and programs to make use of these resources on a continuing basis.

Evidence grows that significant changes lie ahead in our approach to natural resources. Recent concern for new energy sources, elimination of pollution, and the wiser use of natural resources is bringing historic transformations in the thinking of concerned Americans.

PART 4

WOOD IN THE NATION'S FUTURE

Our legacy to the generations still to come is a sound and continually improving management program for our nation's natural resources. (Courtesy U.S. Forest Service)

PROLOG

What might the architects of the industrial revolution have concluded, had they had the foresight to understand all the adverse effects of the mining of coal and metals, of energy intensive mineral processing systems, of industrial pollution, and of the ultimate depletion of non-renewable resources? Perhaps they would have chosen to build a more modest world with greater dependence on materials that can be renewed in perpetuity with a minimum of side effects. A culture and an economy based more broadly on the forests, as was that of this nation before the present century, looks increasingly attractive, especially to young people who stand to suffer most from the mistakes of their predecessors.

It is not too late to change. By trial and error our nation has learned much about population growth, energy, material shortages, pollution, and ecology generally. A better future emphasizing wise use of our natural resources must be planned. No other option exists.

We, the authors, are most optimistic about the future of the United States. We assume that the efforts of the public, research scientists, industrial leaders, and government agencies will be redirected in this century to make provision for a better life for succeeding generations. We assume that the magnitude of the effort will be great; at least comparable to that expended in developing the present system that is beginning to crumble of its own weight. We postulate that forests will continue to grow for the enjoyment and use of future generations. We suggest our need for material goods can be satisfied in large part through the use of wood, which provided so bountifully for the early settlers.

We invite you, the reader, to share our vision of the future progress in wood use by imagining a scientist speaking to us from the year 2076. Caroline Parks Smith, first speaker at a Tricentennial Public Forum, reviews and analyzes the changing wood industry from the perspective of the 21st century. Her expertise centers on the material products our forests provide. Other speakers at this future forum would, of course, speak on the equally important forest benefits of water, wildlife, and wilderness.

W. G. Youngquist
H. O. Fleischer

2076

WOOD UTILIZATION-
A TRICENTENNIAL REVIEW

Caroline Parks Smith

"It is remarkable what a value is still put upon wood even in this age and in this new country — a value more permanent and universal than that of gold." Henry David Thoreau made that discerning observation in the 1850s from his experience at Walden Pond. Thoreau's needs were simple compared to today's, but we have as much reason to subscribe to that statement as did the men and women who preceded us. This historic occasion is an appropriate time to reexamine our dependence on our priceless forest heritage.

Three hundred years ago American life depended heavily on wood — for fuel, for housing, for transportation, and for a myriad of other uses. In 1876 wood continued its indispensable role and contributed to another revolution — the Industrial Revolution — from which this nation emerged as a great world power. One hundred years later wood was still a most important raw material. The annual tonnage of wood produced in the United States in 1976 was greater than the tonnage of steel, cement, plastics, aluminum, and all other metals combined. Each of these three

The author, a materials economist and ecologist, heads the Resources Institute, U. S. Department of Materials and Energy, Washington, D.C. She is widely recognized as an interpreter of scientific and humanitarian progress. This paper was prepared for presentation at the Tricentennial Public Forum on Material Resources and the Environment, Philadelphia, Pa., on July 4, 2076.

eras might well be characterized as an "Age of Wood." But, now in 2076, I feel our claim to that designation is the greatest.

Throughout our history individuals have shown deep concern about the management and use of our natural resources. For the most part, warnings and predictions went unheeded. Changes came but were ineffective in slowing the rapid exploitation of our natural resources. Strangely, about 100 years ago, the realization that an era of abundance was at an end came abruptly. People recognized the growing scarcity of both materials and energy and their increasing dependence on uncertain foreign imports. For the first time the repeated predictions of timber shortages were well documented. No virgin forests stood on the western horizon to exploit. From this complex, manmade dilemma came the great changes that we live with in 2076.

Many changes have led to our present self-sufficiency in wood. I will begin with a comparison of wood use in the bicentennial era with the role of wood in this tricentennial period. Then I will describe changes in the technology of processing and using wood that have extended our timber supply. Many breakthroughs during the last 100 years have made wood the predominant material for the chemical industries. Our forests, nature's bounty, can continue to provide wood, a unique and seemingly limitless material.

Use of Wood — Then and Now

In the early years of the United States sufficient supplies of wood enabled us to use it liberally. Yet only a century ago the annual consumption of wood per capita had declined to barely one metric ton. It had been largely replaced for fuel by gas and petroleum and for other uses by metals, plastics, and masonry. At that time citizens became concerned about the rapidly declining supplies of our nonrenewable materials. Environmental concerns also forced a reassessment of our use of material resources. For example, a report issued in 1973 by the national Commission on Materials Policy classified the major construction materials for "social costs," the added cost in percent of total cost to avoid environmental damage in producing a material. The figures were as follows: lumber, 2; steel, 9; aluminum, 28; and concrete block, 48.

A century ago was, indeed, a time of critical study and introspection! Fortunately for future generations, plans were initiated to control the availability and the use of material resources. Thus in 1975, for example, new Federal legislation provided for an assessment of and a program for renewable resources. But for the development and the partial implementation of these farsighted plans, we could not maintain our standard of living today. As natural petroleum supplies dried up, and as the price of metals climbed with increasing extraction, shipping, and environmental costs, the total volume of wood used began to rise. To meet the growing demands, some major readjustments and changes were necessary.

Even after a long history of ruthless exploitation and primitive forestry practices, timber still grew faster than it was cut in the 20th century. Estimated timber removals in 1970 reached about 400 million cubic meters as compared to 525 million cubic meters annual growth. Those figures were based on what was considered "commercial" — that is, usable by the somewhat wasteful practices of that day. By today's method of measuring total growth, the volumes would, of course, be much higher. The annual removals were mostly (about 70%) in large softwood timber, where imminent shortages were predicted. However, an oversupply of hardwood timber existed, much of it regarded as low quality with sizes and types not wanted by the industrial users of that day.

Integration of the wood-using industries in the 21st century had only begun. Sawtimber, timber-yielding logs of a type and size suitable for sawing into lumber, was overemphasized by today's standards. Fully one-half of the nation's timber went through the sawmill as its primary step for conversion into consumer products. About one-third of the timber cut went to pulpmills, although these mills had progressed to a point at which 35 percent of their supplies came in the form of chipped residues from other manufacturing processes. About 10 percent of the timber cut was made into veneer and plywood products. The remainder was converted into miscellaneous industrial products or burned as fuel.

The entire system of growing, harvesting, selling, and using timber had been set up to accommodate the unintegrated industy as it had developed during the second century of our nation's existence. Sawmillers harvested or purchased sawlogs measured in a lumber unit known as the board foot, which could not readily be converted into measurement units for other products. Pulpmills sought their supplies in roundwood measured by the cord or purchased as chips in tons or cubic feet. Veneer mills were satisfied to select their material from the sawlog supply. Other products, such as poles or ties, were sold by the piece. Only a few large, progressive firms had adopted complete systems of measuring and using their timber supplies in a fully integrated manner. By these systems they greatly minimized their inventory and materials control problems and reduced waste in conversion.

A century ago, as in previous centuries, many still regarded wood as a fuel, a direct source of energy. Most homes and many manufacturing plants generated their heat and energy by direct combustion on the site. Petroleum, a major source of energy then, has now, of course, been replaced by solar and thermal sources; coal, too, is now burned only in central generating plants with pollution controls. Wood today has so many other important uses that it is much too valuable to use as fuel!

Coincident with the change to metric units of measure came a shift from measurement of only the lumber volume of "merchantable" timber to that of the volume of the "complete" tree. This provided a better estimate of the total wood resource and emphasized the portion previously wasted. The net result was a gradual improvement in utilization. Of course, different grades of wood come from the forest; the grades are dependent on whether a wood is suitable for chemicals, fiber, or for some more discriminating use. The economically wasteful practices of processing good sawlogs into pulp or of burning wood residues from the sawmilling process have long since been abandoned. Wood formerly suitable only for fuel is today converted into chemicals and into fiber products. I shall speak more about that later.

By 1976 the trend to convert timber into panel products for specific uses — engineering applications, furniture — became well established. Plywood production had grown at a phenomenal rate and had replaced lumber for many purposes, such as house sheathing for walls, roofs, and subflooring. Structural particleboard, which used wood otherwise suitable only for fiber or fuel, had already been laboratory-tested and was being marketed. Research explored the potential of composite panels or shaped products produced from wood fibers or particles combined with other materials, such as fiberglass and synthetic rubber, or produced from combinations of wood products in forms such as veneer, particles, and paper. These products, each designed to perform functions specified for that particular product, are common today. Most wood-base fiber products of the 21st century are no longer made of virgin roundwood. Following the trend of a century ago, they consist of wood formerly wasted or from recycled, once-used wood or wood-fiber products. Bark and the poorest grades of wood are now used for producing chemicals.

Concurrent with all these changes, the forest products industries, to remain competitive, have made some drastic changes in their practices and products. For many former uses, lumber has been replaced by panels, molded products, and composites. Countless products now being mass-produced in factories — boxes, boats, houses — require well standardized raw materials designed to the particular specifications needed. Lumber, once marketed as a commodity, has largely disappeared. It has been replaced by more sophisticated fabricated and graded products designed for specific uses — solid wood parts, fiber products, and glued composites.

Manufacturers of furniture now use large quantities of particleboard and wood-fiber molded products. Furniture of solid wood is a rare luxury, and not often mass produced. Manufacturers who still produce this type of furniture and similar items obtain their wood supplies not as lumber but as squares or other discrete pieces, each prepared on order. Only craftsmen, hobbyists, woodcarvers, and other specialists who still produce heirloom products by hand, prefer to purchase their supplies directly from a primary lumber processor.

For most wood products in use today, conversion entails chipping, cutting, grinding, tearing, or chemically decomposing wood into small bits or fibers, then reconstituting the material into well designed products. The objectives of our conversion processes are the following: 1) to free the timber user from a need to have timber of great size to get reasonably sized products; 2) to eliminate or reduce weakening effects of knots or areas of irregular grain or other nonuniformities; 3) to improve dimensional stability of wood in use; 4) to reduce waste in processing; and 5) to develop more efficient processes of drying wood, treating wood with chemicals, and getting wood into the most efficient shape for an intended use.

In reviewing our historic timber situation, I noted a preference for large, softwood sawtimber of "good quality," and an overabundance of unused hardwood timber. Meanwhile, softwoods were being rapidly depleted. This situation has, of course, been remedied. Use of some hardwoods for lumber often presented problems in drying and in fastening, especially the irregular pieces of denser woods so common in hardwood timber stands a century ago. These problems, however, were eliminated through adopting new conversion processes. Already in use for paper a century ago, hardwoods now commonly provide fiber and particle products for the construction and other industries. The concern about converting hardwood timber stands to softwood stands is no longer valid. All wood supplies regardless of preconceived preferences about species, size, or quality find useful and profitable outlets.

Technical Changes—A Boon to Wood Users

Technical improvements through research and industrial development have come about rapidly since Americans acknowledged the importance of wood to the economy. Without this dedication to wise use of our forests, we would not have the versatile wood products on which we depend. A century ago a builder accepted wood for construction largely in its original form. Processing methods now produce wood in shapes and sizes desired by architects and engineers. Large panels and extruded or molded shapes such as beams, columns, tubes, and curved members are all available. Rearrangement of wood elements in reconstituted products gives products stability, freedom from shrinkage, swelling, and warping, and the needed combination of strength properties. Current processing methods impart fire resistance to wood by adding minute quantities of chemicals to dampen the combustion process. By removing the elements essential to the growth of the organisms causing deterioration, wood now resists attacks by insects and decaying organisms without adding toxics.

Long before 1976 we knew how to "explode" the cellulose fiber to produce hardboard panels without the addition of adhesives. Since then, we have learned to manipulate the behavior of wood and also how to modify it nondestructively. We now make "softwoods" out of "hardwoods" and low-density products of great strength from wood fibers. The major end-accomplishment is the ability to make, within limits, wood materials of any desired strength or density. The disadvantages that hampered the utilization of our dense hardwood a century ago are gone!

Now we can bond pieces of wood together without adding expensive synthetic adhesives by a partial and temporary treatment of wood to dissolve the surface structure. This development is related to our understanding of lignin, a component of wood. This new process allows us to join pieces of wood together by a process comparable to that of welding metals! Since this breakthrough, we have been freed from limitations of size and shape to develop limitless shapes from wood at will.

Wood—The Material for 21st Century Chemical Industry

Nature has designed a remarkable method for creating organic materials from carbon, oxygen, and hydrogen, with the aid of solar energy. Plants daily use this process called photosynthesis on which all other living matter depends. The wild forest, growing at a very moderate rate of two metric tons of organic material per hectare per year, produces three times as much cellulose fiber per year as does a good crop of cotton.

In the early wood chemical industry, wood was not used directly for chemical production. Some useful products such as acetic acid and methanol were recovered from the charcoal process. Naval stores yielded turpentine and pitch; tall oil was extracted from waste liquor left from the pulping of southern pines. Research, at that time, showed how to regulate the production of these chemicals by treating the living tree. Only minor constitutents of wood were extracted for direct chemical use.

The true wood chemical industry began with the advent of processes to use the major constituents of wood—cellulose and lignin—for chemical products. The cellulose fiber is composed of giant molecular chains, or polymers, just like cotton cellulose, although not so long. Cellulose is a highly useful chemical material. The highest polymer fractions can be dissolved and reconstituted into fibers such as rayon or converted into cellulose acetate, esters, and ethers, and these in turn into explosives, plastics, and lacquers.

Cellulose converts chemically into sugar and alcohol, then into heavy chemicals. Nonedible as well as some edible sugars are produced and used as the basis for manufacturing protein yeasts or alcohol. Although these processes have long been known, until recently they were never fully exploited. Now we can convert trees quickly and directly into oil through the cyclic application of heat and pressure in the presence of a catalyst. Thus, we duplicate nature's process of making oil in a fraction of the time. Plastics, motor fuel, and many other chemicals formerly produced from petroleum are now made from wood once wasted.

As mentioned earlier, understanding the nature of lignin was crucial to advancing our knowledge of wood chemistry. Lignin, the binding material between the cellulose fibers, makes up 25 to 30 percent of wood. As a result of major research, this plastic binding material between wood fibers can now be dissolved from wood for use or modified in place. As a byproduct of the cellulose pulping industry, lignin provides the basic material for plastics and for much of the post-petroleum chemical industry. By modifying lignin within wood structure, then by bending or by otherwise shaping, by stretching, or by compressing the cellulose structure, followed by fixing the lignin, wood can now be molded like a plastic or bent, stamped, or drawn like a metal.

Wood—The Renewable Material

Throughout history people have expressed grave concern about whether America could meet future needs for timber, our major renewable material resource. The 20th century has gone down in history as the most splendid and also the most wasteful period on this planet. Much speculation anticipated the imminent doom sure to follow the ultimate depletion of the world's nonrenewable resources. Only very late in the century did we actually turn from speculation to an attack on material and energy problems.

Today in 2076 all citizens bear witness to their willingness to live within a materials budget. We have learned to "make do" with what we have, in the quantities available. And, fortunately, we have learned to appreciate, to manage, and to enlarge our major renewable resource—wood. Wasteful processing methods, extravagant habits of artificially created obsolescence, and unsightly wood junkyards of the previous century have disappeared.

A century ago we had made only a start on improving the efficiency of our processing methods to produce higher yields of wood products. Sawmill efficiency improved through many steps. From the circular saw the industry went to thin bandsaws; from manual control of the sawing process to computerized control. More precise and dependable equipment resulted in greater accuracy and increased yields. In lumber-drying, we developed methods of rapidly removing water without creating shrinkage flaws.

In the chemical-pulping processes predominant in the 20th century, pulp yields were as low as 45 to 50 percent. Major components of wood, lignin and degraded cellulose, were lost or converted into process fuel in the chemical recovery process. When changes in methods saved the portion of cellulose that had been degraded, pulp yields soared to 65 or even 70 percent. Of course the solution of the "lignin mystery"—which I have already mentioned—provided a new material for industrial conversion that accounted for almost one-third of all pulped wood.

Great increases in wood supply came from using species not used before. Many American woods considered "refractory" or "weed species" in 1876 had already been proved economically valuable by 1976, such as aspen and cottonwood, sweetgum and tupelo, and hemlock and the true firs. Equipment changes enabled small stems formerly left to rot in the woods to be used for sawmilling, for veneer and plywood, and for pulp manufacture. Economic changes in the value of raw materials generally made it profitable to bring from the woods kinds and qualities of wood not formerly used, such as insect-killed or partially decayed wood, limbs, broken and irregular pieces, and even bark. Although these irregular materials were at first not sought, changes made their use feasible.

Our pulp industry receives much of its raw material in the form of chips rather than roundwood. The industry has avidly sought chips from wastewood generated in other primary processing industries such as sawmilling and veneer and plywood manufacture. As the industries in turn have improved their efficiencies and generated less waste, the pulp, paper, and fiberboard industries expanded the recycling of once-used wood gathered in the form of old paperboard containers, newspapers, and even once-used timber, poles, ties, and demolition waste from urban trash.

Recycled wood fiber, used at a level of about 20 percent a century ago, readily rose to the present level of about 50 percent. Today recycling all types of used materials is considered essential. Structural fiberboards—fine materials for construction because of their strength, stiffness, insulating properties—are the long term resting place of much wood fiber material first used in paper or as solid wood.

Throughout our history the largest single use of wood has been in the construction of houses and other buildings. Only construction practices and materials used have changed. Americans do not have to visit a museum to see the homes of their ancestors. Many still stand and are being used—a great tribute to the durability of wood. No doubt some in this audience live in the beautiful houses dating from our bicentennial or, perhaps, from our centennial period. Our most severe criticism of them is the lavish use of wood! Because of the large volume of wood used in construction, a great amount of research has continually been directed toward improving wood utilization in this field. The growing practice of designing wood-base products for specific uses has resulted in great improvements in utilization. For example, high-grade lumber was almost universally used for sheathing buildings a century and a half ago. The panel industry changed that, and made the use of thinner panel materials possible—half the thickness of the lumber then used—to sheath buildings. Actually, these materials improved the strength and rigidity of a structure.

Today's unit has greater fire safety, requires much less energy, and is in all other respects as liveable and durable as the house a century ago. New methods of evaluating structural adequacy of completed structures, rather than smaller building components, revealed areas for which savings in materials could be made. The savings achieved also extend to our larger structure—but to a lesser degree.

A century ago much research on the use of adhesives concentrated on procedures to make wood members larger and more functional than nature could supply them. A thriving laminating industry supplied large timbers as needed, either straight or curved, each designed and assembled of moderate-size pieces of lumber, to meet specific stress requirements. More modern adhesives have made possible advancements far beyond earlier levels in producing required or specified shapes and sizes of wood from a great variety of species and qualities of wood. All this has been via fiber or particle processes. The development of structural particleboard a century ago was just a prelude to a major industry that today supplies large members that are glued, shaped, or molded to meet architects' and engineers' requirements.

The multifold changes in wood-material demands is reflected in forest operations. Two centuries ago when the magnificent white pine stands of the Lake States were cut down, only the large sawlogs were harvested for lumber. Years later the same land was recut, but by that time pulpwood—roundwood of very moderate size down to about 8 centimeters top diameter—was extracted. Timber harvesting today is fully mechanized. As fiber and particle products began to predominate in the wood industry, wood was more and more dismembered in the forest. Entire trees are chipped for delivery to processing plants. Only a predetermined small percentage of a tree—twigs, leaves, roots—are left in a forest to provide ground protection and to recycle the essential mineral nutrients needed for the next crop of timber. In areas of high-intensity forestry, it is profitable to replace the mineral nutrients through fertilization when a new crop is established.

This brings me to the function of the forester, whose responsibility is the management of our nation's woodlands. Wise management supplies us with continuing crops of timber as well as providing for the many other uses of the forest, such as watershed, wildlife, recreation, and aesthetic values. A century ago, wood grew essentially as a wild plant in the forest, like grains and fruits grew before intensive agriculture developed. Just as we have succeeded in multiplying the yields of grains per hectare by applying scientific developments to agriculture, so have we succeeded increasing the growth of wood crops by employing scientific and intensive forestry practices.

A century ago, forestry researchers had demonstrated that the growth rate of trees, in terms of wood laid down in the stem, could be doubled through particular genetic selection and breeding practices. By using genetic strains of trees displaying particular characteristics desired, the amount of wood grown during the first generation could be doubled. Since then we have progressed further. On selected hectares designated especially for growing timber crops for harvest, fertilizing and irrigating produces another doubling of growth rate.

At one time the question of how large should timber be grown for harvest was hotly debated among foresters. The development of durable and economical wood-bonding processes frees us from the need to use wood as nature provides it. We now supply improved products regardless of size. Nevertheless, applying intensive and expensive forestry practices speeds the growing process greatly.

Economic considerations usually predominate in determining rotation periods for forests. Added to initial investment cost is interest on the investment over the many years of a tree's life. Therefore, high-intensity forests managed for the single wood crop are usually short-rotation forests. These intensively managed lands, often with periodically repeated investments in fertilizer, irrigation, and highly selected expensive planting stock, are usually not grown to great size over many years. Wood for conversion to fiber or chemicals now requires from 3 to 7 years under the best growth conditions. On most commercial forest lands, management, while striving for high timber yields, is modified to secure the many other essential benefits forests provide—watershed, wildlife, recreation, and aesthetic values. All areas are carefully considered and each area is handled to secure an optimum mix of these "products" in addition to the wood that can be produced.

The very careful management of "production" forests, coupled with high standards of wood utilization, enable us to meet our raw material needs. We have not sacrificed the other equally important values we associate with forests. In addition, intensive management on selected areas gives us the unique opportunity of preserving large and widely distributed areas in an undeveloped state much as they were when first viewed by our ancestors. The cultural and the scientific contributions of these wilderness areas have been immense.

I mentioned that wood fiber material is salvaged from urban trash. It should not be overlooked that trees grown for shade and beautification in urban parks and residential areas also form an important source of material for industry. These trees eventually die or must be removed and replaced for some other reason. The chipped material, formerly burned, is fed into the industrial production system for conversion into particleboards, fiber products, and chemicals. Thus, land that may originally have been part of the base of about 200 million hectares of commercial U.S. timberland, but subsequently preempted for other developments, continues to contribute to our wood material supplies.

An area in which improvement has not depended primarily on the forester has been the attitude of the landowner and of the general public toward land use. As our country developed, some of its best timber-growing land was converted into farmland. On farms a wooded area was often reserved to provide fuelwood and occasional logs for market. About one-fourth of the best timber-growing land was in these small farm woodlots. Another even larger segment, 33 percent, was held in small tracts by a variety of owners who had little knowledge of or interest in forestry. The problem of the appalling losses to our economy from the former neglect of these productive hectares has, of course, been remedied. Production from this timberland has been effectively doubled during the last century.

Past, Present, and Future

Now let me attempt to recapitulate the U.S. timber situation, past, present, and future. Quantitative data about our country's renewable resources is regularly reported to Congress at 10-year intervals. In my opinion, the beginning of the modern forestry-planning era began with the passage by Congress of the Forest and Rangeland Renewable Resources Planning Act of 1974. Our population of about 210 million people was then enjoying the use of about 1 metric ton of wood per person per year; this tonnage was extracted mostly from natural stands of timber by rather primitive methods and processed and used without much thought to full utilization. In fact, one of the period's chief forest industrialists referred to his coworkers and colleagues as "wastrels."

Since 1976, our population has doubled, the land area

available for commercially growing timber has shrunk, and wood has filled the gap left by our depleted, nonrenewable resources. Roughly 800 million metric tons of wood are now used annually in consumer products. On an average, we grow five metric tons per year of wood per hectare of commercial timberland on which we claim we practice high-intensity forestry. This is not a miraculous achievement for in 1976 some foresters already proposed that such a goal was realistic even with their limited knowledge and tools!

We still have much to do, since we have scarcely kept abreast of consumer demands. Let me list a few methods that will greatly improve our resource situation; any one if pursued agressively by research and application will bring results.

> Intensify forestry practices in natural stands through cultural operations to bring about full stocking; improve cuttings and thinnings; provide full fire protection; protect against insects and disease.
>
> Grow wood more rapidly and of better quality by selecting superior species and fast-growing trees and incorporating genetic improvements.
>
> Adopt sound forestry practices on U.S. commercial timberland privately held in farms and small tracts.
>
> Increase the recycling of previously used wood fiber products.
>
> Improve product performance so that wood products last longer through improved design.
>
> Design products — especially engineering structures — so that structures can be efficiently constructed with less wood.
>
> Expand practice of rehabilitating existing structures to meet new needs.

I wish to share with you an historic assessment of what is attainable for wood as predicted in 1949 by Dr. Egon Glesinger, then Head of the Forestry Division of the Food and Agriculture Organization of the United Nations. At that time, Dr. Glesinger published an imaginative book entitled *The Coming Age of Wood* in which he predicted many of the developments that we enjoy today. Speaking on a global basis, he concluded:

> Forests can be made to produce about fifty times their present volume of end products and still remain a permanently self-renewing source for our raw material

supplies. We have progressed, but we still have much to accomplish before attaining that objective![1]

If I were asked what is the greatest single achievement in the last century for wiser use of our wood resource, I would have to pass over the many brilliant scientific achievements. What stands out as the most remarkable is the change in the attitude of our citizens! We are more conservation conscious. We have become intolerant of waste. Willingly we pay the social and the economic costs of the improvements needed to use our resources more wisely. We acknowledge the significance of the forest in the spiritual and material life of Americans.

In the future our descendants will pause and look back on American history as we are doing now. What will life be like then and how will we be judged on our management of America's resources? I suggest that the greatest legacy we can leave to the generations still to come is a sound and continually improving management program for our nation's natural resources.

Authors' Note: The foregoing picture of wood utilization in the year 2076 is based on predictions 100 years earlier. Obviously, change will come, and only change for the better is in keeping with our nation's tradition.

NOTES

Part 1: Wood in the New Nation, 1776

[1]Allen H. Eaton, *Handicrafts of New England* (New York:Harper, 1949), p. 27.

[2]Thomas Anbury, *Travels Through the Interior Parts of America, in a Series of Letters by an Officer*, Vol. I, rep. of 1789 ed. (New York:Arno, 1969), pp. 324-325.

[3]Daniel Neal, *History of New England to Year of Our Lord, 1700*, 2 vols., rep. of 1747 ed. (A.M.S. Press, Inc.: New York, 1976).

[4]Carl Bridenbaugh, *Cities in Revolt: Urban Life in America 1743-1776* (New York:Knopf, 1955), pp. 232-233.

[5]Ibid. p. 232.

[6]Mark J. Boesch, 1974. "Americas," *Forest and History* 26(1):17-22, 1974.

[7]Jenks Cameron, *The Development of Government Forest Control in the United States* (Baltimore:Johns Hopkins, 1928), p. 17.

[8]Edwin M. Betts, ed., *Thomas Jefferson's Farm Book* (Princeton:Princeton Univ. Press, 1953), p. 339.

[9]Charles H. Sherrill, *French Memories of Eighteenth-Century America* (New York:Scribners, 1915), p. 282.

[10]Jacques P. Brissot DeWarville, *New Travels in the United States of America*, trans. Mara Soceanu Vamos and Durand Echeverria, ed. Durand Echeverria, (Cambridge:Harvard Univ. Press. 1964), p. 155.

[11]Sherrill, op. cit. p. 301.

[12]Eric Sloane, *A Reverence for Wood* (New York: Funk, 1965), p. 75.

[13]Ibid. p. 71.

Part 2: Wood in the Growing Nation, 1876

[1]Victor S. Clark, *History of Manufacturers in the U.S., from 1607-1928,* Vol. II (New York:Peter Smith, 1949), p. 127.

[2]Jenks Cameron, *The Development of Governmental Forest Control in the United States* (Baltimore:Johns Hopkins, 1928), p. 135.

[3]Franklin B. Hough, *Report on Forestry* (Washington, D.C.:U.S. Govt. Print. Off., 1878), p. 16.

[4]Richard F. Lillard, *The Great Forest* (New York:Knopf, 1947), p. 148.

[5]Walt Whitman, *The Portable Walt Whitman,* Mark Van Doren, ed. (New York:Viking, 1945), p. 178.

Part 3: Wood in the Industrial Era, 1976

[1]Charles A. Nelson, *History of the Forest Products Laboratory (1910-1963),* USDA Forest Serv. (Madison, Wis.: Forest Prod. Lab., 1971), p. 23.

[2]John J. Kuenzel, "Ships — 100 Years in Retrospect," In *Proceedings of Wood Symposium—One Hundred Years of Engineering Progress with Wood,* Timber Eng. Co. (Washington, D.C.:1952), pp. 46-49.

[3]*The Outlook for Timber in the United States,* USDA Forest Res. Rep. No. 20 (Washington, D.C.:1973), p. 20.

[4]Charles W. Bingham (Weyerhaeuser Co.), "The Keynote," *Forest Prod. J.* 21(9):9-14, 1975.

[5]Vernon L. Robinson, "An Estimate of Technological Progress in the Lumber and Wood Products Industry," *Forest Sci.* 21(6):149-154, 1975.

Part 4: Wood in the Nation's Future, 2076

[1]Egon Glesinger, *The Coming of Age of Wood* (New York: Simon and Schuster, 1949).

REFERENCES

Part 1: Wood in the New Nation, 1776

Adams, Ruth. *Pennsylvania Dutch Art*. Cleveland:World Pub., 1950.

Anbury, Thomas. *Travels Through the Interior Parts of America in a Series of Letters by an Officer*, 2 vols. (rep. of 1789 ed.) New York:Arno, 1969.

Betts, Edwin M., ed. *Thomas Jefferson's Farm Book*. Princeton: Princeton Univ. Press, 1953.

Beyer, Glen H. *Housing and Society*. New York:MacMillan, 1965.

Bishop, Robert. *American Folk Sculpture*. New York:Dutton, 1974.

Boesch, Mark. "Americas." *Forest and History* 26(9):17-22, 1974.

Bolles, Albert S. *Industrial History of the United States*. Norwich, Conn.: Henry Bill, 1881.

Bridenbaugh, Carl. *Cities in Revolt: Urban Life in American 1743-1776*. New York:Knopf, 1955.

Brissot DeWarville, Jean P. *New Travels in the United States of America*, trans. Mara Soceanu Vamos and Durand Echeverria, ed. Durand Echeverria. Cambridge:Harvard Univ. Press, 1964.

Brown, Ralph H. *Historical Geography of the United States*, ed. J. Russell Whitaker. New York:Harcourt, 1948.

Burchard, John, and Albert Bush-Brown. *The Architecture of America: A Social and Cultural History*. Boston:Little, 1961.

Cameron, Jenks. *The Development of Governmental Forest Control in the United States*. Baltimore:Johns Hopkins, 1928.

Chapelle, Howard. *The History of American Sailing Ships*. New York: Norton:1935.

Coombs, Charles. *High Timber: The Story of American Forestry.* Cleveland:World Pub., 1960.

Dana, Samuel. *Forest and Range Policy: Its Development in the U.S.* New York:McGraw, 1956.

Debo, Angie. *A History of the Indians of the United States.* Norman, Okla.: Univ. of Okla. Press, 1970.

DeFebaugh, James E. *History of the Lumber Industry of America,* Vol. I. Chicago:American Lumberman, 1906.

Drepperd, Carl William. *American Clocks and Clockmakers.* New York:Doubleday, 1947.

Earle, Alice. *Home Life in Colonial Days,* ed. Shirley Glubok. New York:MacMillan, 1969.

Eaton, Allen H. *Handicrafts of New England.* New York:Harper, 1949.

Eberlein, Harold D. *The Architecture of Colonial America.* Boston:Little, 1915.

Cortland V. D. Hubbard. *American Georgian Architecture.* Bloomington:Ind. Univ. Press, 1952.

Edwards, Ruth M. *American Indians of Yesteryear.* San Antonio, Texas:Naylor, 1948.

Fitch, James Marston. *American Building: The Forces That Shape It.* Boston:Houghton, 1948.

Foley, Daniel J., and Priscilla S. Lord. *The Folk Arts and Crafts of New England.* Radnor, Pa.:Chilton, 1965.

Furnas, Joseph C. *The Americans: A Social History of the United States, 1587-1914.* New York:Putnam, 1969.

Gould, Mary E. *Early American Woodenware,* 2d ed. Springfield, Mass.: Pond Ekberg, 1948.

————. *The Early American House.* New York:Medill McBride, 1949.

Greene, Evarts B. "The History of American Life," *Revolutionary Generation, 1763-1790,* Vol. IV. New York:McMillan, 1943.

Hutchins, John G. B. *The American Maritime Industries and Public Policy.* New York:Russell, 1969.

Inverarity, Robert B. *Art of the Northwest Coast Indians.* Berkeley: Univ. of Calif. Press, 1950.

Ise, John. *The United States Forest Policy.* New Haven, Conn.: Yale Univ. Press, 1920.

Ketchum, William C., Jr. *American Basketry and Woodenware.* New York: McMillan, 1974.

Klingberg, Frank S. *The Morning of America.* New York:Appleton-Century, 1941.

Laing, Alexander. *American Sailing Ships,* ed. Mayor Alfred. New York: McGraw, 1971.

Lavine, Sigmund A. *Handmade in America: The Heritage of Colonial Craftsmen.* New York:Dodd, 1966.

Lillard, Richard, G. *The Great Forest.* New York:Knopf, 1947.

Lipman, Jean. *American Folk Art in Wood, Metal, and Stone.* New York: Dover, 1969.

Lord, Eleanor L. *Industrial Experiments in the British Colonies of North America.* Baltimore:Johns Hopkins, 1898.

Newcomb, Rexford. *Spanish Colonial Architecture in the U.S.* Locust Valley, N.Y.: J. J. Augustin, 1957.

Nicholson, Katherine S. *Historic American Trees.* New York:Frye, 1922.

Oliver, John W. *History of American Technology.* New York:Ronald, 1956.

Pinckney, Pauline A. *American Figureheads and their Carvers.* New York: Norton, 1940.

Rawlings, James S. *Virginia's Colonial Churches: Architectural Guide.* Richmond:Garrett, 1963.

Rawson, Marion N. *When Antiques Were Young.* New York:Dutton, 1931.

_____. *Handwrought Ancestors: The Story of Early American Shops and Those who Worked Therein.* New York:Dutton, 1936.

Robinson, Ethel, and Thomas Robinson. *Houses in America.* New York:Viking, 1936.

Rogers, Meyric R. *American Interior Design.* New York:Norton, 1947.

Rose, Harold W. *The Colonial Houses of Worship in America.* New York:Hastings, 1963.

Schonler, James. *Americans of 1776.* New York:Dodd, 1906.

Shalkop, Robert. *Wooden Saints.* Feldafing, Germany:Buckhein Verlag, 1967.

Sherrill, Charles H. *French Memories of Eighteenth-Century America.* New York: Scribners, 1915.

Shumway, George, et al. *Conestoga Wagon 1750-1850: Freight Carrier for 100 years of America's Westward Expansion.* York, Pa.:Shumway, 1966.

Sloane, Eric. *A Reverence for Wood.* New York:Funk, 1965.

Smith, Herbert A. *Forest and Forestry in the United States,* U.S. Dept. of Agri. Washington, D.C.: U.S. Govt. Print. Off., 1922.

Stout, John J. *Early Pennsylvania Arts and Crafts.* New York:Barnes, 1964.

Tunis, Edwin. *Colonial Living.* Cleveland, Ohio:World Pub., 1957.

Underhill, Ruth M. *Red Man's America.* Chicago:Univ. of Chicago Press, 1971.

Winters, Robert K. *The Forest and Man.* New York:Vantage, 1974.

Part 2: Wood in the Growing Nation, 1876

Allen, Richard S. *Covered Bridges of the Northeast.* Brattleboro, Vt.: Stephen Greene, 1957.

Andrews, Wayne. *Architecture in America*. Paterson, N.J.:Atheneum, 1960.

Archibald, Raymond. "A Survey of Timber Highway Bridges in the United States." In *Proceedings of Wood Symposium—One Hundred Years of Progress with Wood*. Timber Eng. Co., pp. 34-45. Washington, D.C.:1952.

Brewington, Marion V. *Shipcarvers of North America*. Barre, Mass.:Barre, 1962.

Butler, Joseph T. *American Antiques, 1800-1900: A Collector's History and Guide*. New York:Odyssey, 1965.

Cameron, Jenks. *The Development of Governmental Forest Control in the United States*. Baltimore:Johns Hopkins, 1928.

Chaney, Charles A. "Shore Structures—Improvement in Structures." In *Proceedings of Wood Symposium—One Hundred Years of Engineering Progress with Wood*. Timber Eng. Co., pp. 50-56. Washington, D.C.:1952.

Clark, Victor S. *History of Manufactures in the United States, from 1607-1928*, Vol. II. New York:Peter Smith, 1949.

Defenbaugh, James E. *History of the Lumber Industry in America*, Vol. I. Chicago:The American Lumberman, 1906.

Doig, Ivan. "John J. McGilvra and Timber Trespass." *Forest History* 13(4):7, 1970.

Dunbar, Seymour. *A History of Travel in America*, 4 vols. Indianapolis:Bobbs Merrill, 1915.

Durrenberger, J. A. *Turnpikes: A Study of the Toll Road Movement in the Middle Atlantic States and Maryland*. Valdosta, Ga.; J. A. Durrenberger, 1931.

Freeman, Ruth, and Larry Freeman. *Victorian Furniture*. Watkin's Glen, N.Y.: Century House, 1950.

Furnas, Joseph C. *The Americans: A Social History of the United States, 1587-1914*. New York:Putnam, 1969.

Hardwood Plywood Institute. *The Story of Hardwood Plywood,* pamphlet. Arlington, Va.: n.d.

Hough, Franklin B. *Report on Forestry*. U.S. Govt. Print. Off. Washington, D.C.:1878.

Hunt, George W. "A Century of Engineering in Wood Preservation." In *Proceedings of Wood Symposium—One Hundred Years of Engineering Progress with Wood*. Timber Eng. Co., pp. 66-69. Washington, D.C.:1952.

Hutchins, John. *The American Maritime Industries and Public Policy, 1789-1914: An Economic History*, repr. of 1941 ed. New York:Russell, 1969.

Klamkin, Marian, and Charles Klamkin. *Wood Carvings: North American Folk Sculptures*. New York:Hawthorn, 1974.

Kuenzel, John G. "Ships — One Hundred Years in Retrospect." In *Proceedings of Wood Symposium—One Hundred Years of Progress With Wood.* Timber Eng. Co., pp. 46-49. Washington, D.C.:1952.

Labatut, Jean, and W. J. Lane, eds. *Highways in our National Life.* Princeton, N.J.:Princeton Univ. Press, 1950.

Lantz, Louise K. *Old American Kitchenware, 1725-1925.* Nashville, Tenn.:Nelson, 1970.

Lavine, Sigmund A. *Handmade in America: The Heritage of Colonial Craftsmen.* New York:Dodd, 1966.

Lillard, Richard G. *The Great Forest.* New York:Knopf, 1947.

Lindley, Kenneth. *The Woodblock Engravers.* New York:Drake, 1970.

Lipman, Jean. *American Folk Art in Wood, Metal, and Stone.* New York:Dover, 1948.

Maass, John. *The Victorian Home in America.* New York:Hawthorn, 1972.

Meyer, Balthaser, H. *History of Transportation in the United States Before 1860.* Washington, D.C.:Peter Smith, 1948.

Oliver, John W. *History of American Technology.* New York:Ronald, 1956.

Ringwalt, John L. *Development of Transportation in the United States, 1888.* New York:Johnson Reprint, 1967.

Sloane, Eric. *A Reverence for Wood.* New York:Funk, 1965.

Smith, David. *History of Papermaking in the United States (1961-1969).* New York:Lockwood, 1970.

Wangaard, Frederick F. "A Brief History of the American Forest Products Industries." In *Proceedings of Wood Symposium—One Hundred Years of Engineering Progress With Wood.* Timber Eng. Co., pp. 100-106. Washington, D.C.:1952.

Weeks, Lyman H. *A History of Paper Manufacturing in the United States, 1690-1916.* New York:Burt Franklin, 1916.

Whiffen, Marcus. *American Architecture Since 1780: A Guide to the Styles.* Cambridge, Mass.: MIT Press, 1969.

Yates, Raymond F., and Marguerite W. Yates. *A Guide to Victorian Antiques.* New York:Harper, 1949.

Part 3: Wood in the Industrial Era, 1976

Bingham, Charles, W. "The Keynote." *Forest Prod. J.* 21(9):9-14, 1975.

Kuenzel, John. "Ships—100 Years in Retrospect." In *Proceedings of Wood Symposium—One-Hundred Years of Progress With Wood.* Timber Eng. Co., pp. 46-49, Washington, D.C.:1952.

Nelson, Charles A. *History of the Forest Products Laboratory (1910-1963).* Madison, Wis.:USDA Forest Serv., Forest Prod. Lab., 1971.

Phelps, Robert B., and Dwight Hair. *The Demand and Price Situation for Forest Products 1973-74,* USDA Forest Serv. Misc. Publ. No. 1292., Washington, D.C.: U.S. Govt. Print. Off., 1974.

President's Advisory Panel on Timber and the Environment. Washington, D.C.:U.S. Govt. Print. Off., 1973.

Robinson, Vernon L. "An Estimate of Technological Progress in the Lumber and Wood-Products Industry." *Forest Sci.* 21(2):149-154, 1975.

Timber Engineering Company. *Proceedings of Wood Symposium—One Hundred Years of Engineering Progress With Wood,* Timber Eng. Co. Washington, D.C.:1952.

The Outlook for Timber in the United States, USDA Forest Serv. Res. Rep. No. 20. Washington, D.C.:U.S. Govt. Print. Off., 1973.

A Summary of the Program and Assessment for the Nation's Renewable Resources as Required by the Forest and Range and Renewable Resources Planning Act of 1974. USDA Forest Serv. Washington, D.C.:Govt. Print. Off., 1975.

U.S. Department of Commerce. *Preliminary Rep. MC72 (P)-1.* Washington, D.C.:U.S. Govt. Print. Off., 1974.

Part 4: Wood in the Nation's Future, 2076

Glesinger, Egon. *The Coming of Age of Wood.* New York:Simon and Schuster, 1949.